For Colin

ACKNOWLEDGMENTS

The paragraph beginning on page 47 with "J. K. Fairbank . . ." is quoted from EAST ASIA: THE GREAT TRADITION, by Edwin O. Reischauer and John K. Fairbank (Boston: Houghton Mifflin Company, 1958)
The sentence beginning on page 130 "It is an undoubted fact . . ." is quoted from THE WESTERN WORLD AND JAPAN, by Sir George Sansom (London: The Cresset Press, 1950)

The sentence beginning on page 94 "The Manchus owed their . . ." is from ANNALS AND MEMOIRS OF THE COURT OF PEKING, by E. Backhouse and J. O. P. Bland (London: Wm. Heinemann, 1914)

IN A CLEAR, LIMPID STYLE, and with the accuracy and insight that come from many years of living in and studying the area about which she writes, Peter Lum offers a brilliant panorama of the events and the men who created the East Asian world we must live with today.

From approximately the middle of the thirteenth to the middle of the fourteenth centuries, the nightmare of Mongol power weighed heavily on the conquered peoples of East Asia and a large part of Europe. But in the year 1368, a revolt, beginning in Peking, drove the Mongols out of China back to the deserts whence they had come. A brilliant new Chinese dynasty, the Ming, ruled the Middle Kingdom again, bringing peace, prosperity, and a new flowering of art, science and literature to the Empire. But the fear and hatred that Mongol rule had generated would persist for centuries and play a decisive role in the attitudes of the peoples of China, Japan and Korea towards all foreigners.

In the West, the increasing wealth and power of the nation states sparked a period of exploration and expansion that brought the first confrontations between the West and East. The early attempts by merchant/explorers and Jesuit priests to open trade routes and advance Christianity were met with distrust and hostility, with the result that the great civilizations of the East remained isolated and unaware of the major changes taking place in the world balance of power.

Peter Lum tells the history of East Asia in the turbulent 600 years from the fourteenth century to 1912 when the last of the Dynasties that had ruled China for thousands of years crumbled, and the Chinese Republic of Sun Yat-sen came into being. Rich in anecdotes, with many photographs, maps, drawings and chronological charts, her narrative encompasses the many facets of each country's history and culture, continually emphasizing and clarifying their influence on each other and on the rest of the world.

by the same author

STARS IN OUR HEAVEN

FABULOUS BEASTS

ITALIAN FAIRY TALES

FAIRY TALES FROM THE BARBARY COAST

THE GROWTH OF CIVILIZATION IN EAST ASIA

SIX CENTURIES IN EAST ASIA

揮狂屠牛説邂逅総土東海
老黄公
千今改息横行者誰識人中
此額同
甲午南善

"Tiger," Korean Painting, 18th century.
NATIONAL MUSEUM OF KOREA

SIX CENTURIES IN EAST ASIA

China, Japan and Korea from

the 14th Century to 1912

PETER LUM

S. G. PHILLIPS   New York

Library of Congress Cataloging in Publication Data

Lum, Peter, 1911-
    Six centuries in East Asia.

    SUMMARY: Surveys the history of China, Japan, and Korea from the
end of the Mongol Empire in the fourteenth century to the founding of
the Chinese Republic in 1912.
    Bibliography: p.
    1. East (Far East)—Civilization—Juvenile literature. [1. China—History.
2. Japan—History. 3. Korea—History. 4. East (Far East)—Civilization]
I. Title.
DS509.3.L82   915′.03   72-12582
ISBN 0-87599-183-1

CONTENTS

LIST OF ILLUSTRATIONS

LIST OF MAPS

SIX CENTURIES IN EAST ASIA

A WORD OF WARNING, WHICH MAY

FURTHER CONFUSE THE READER

IT IS HARD to be consistent in spelling Chinese or Japanese names, or, indeed, those of any Oriental language. It is also sometimes difficult to date historical events exactly in our calendar, and the earlier the date the more difficult it may be.

To take the question of dates first. Before the Chinese Republic officially adopted the Western calendar in 1912, the Chinese used a twelve-month lunar calendar, counting months from one new moon to the next. This slipped backwards in relation to the solar calendar of 365¼ days by about eleven days a year, a difficulty the Chinese solved by inserting a sort of "leap-month" every few years, so that there would be two second months, or two fifth, or two eighth months. The New

Year was the second new moon after the winter solstice, falling somewhere between January 21 and February 19, so that some dates were in a new year according to Western reckoning but still in the old year according to the Chinese.

The Chinese did not reckon years from any one date of religious significance, such as the birth of Christ in the Christian calendar, or Mohammed's flight to Medina in the Moslem calendar, but from the accession of an emperor. They also counted days, and later, years, in cycles of sixty, an ancient system which is said to have been in use since the third millennium B.C.

It is thus only for our own convenience that we write of events as taking place in the second century B.C., for instance, or the eighteenth century A.D., and even then the date of an event may vary by a year.

Two different dates for a dynasty or a shogunate coming to power may both be correct. The Manchus reckoned their dynasty from 1636 but it was not until 1644 that they replaced the Ming Dynasty in China. The Ashikaga Shogunate dates from 1336, but it was 1392 before a civil war over the succession was settled. Nobunaga's rise to power can be dated from several critical events.

When it comes to language, we should remember that the script used by the Chinese and Japanese is written in characters, or ideograms, and that the words expressed by these characters may be spelled in different ways when they are romanized— that is to say, when they are reproduced in a western alphabetical script. Not only will a word be romanized differently in different western languages, English, French or German for example, but even in the same language no one spelling is necessarily correct. Nor does any one spelling necessarily reproduce the Chinese or Japanese sounds accurately, because these sounds are so unlike those of European languages that different Europeans may hear them quite differently.

Further complications arise from regional variations. The written Chinese script is, of course, the same everywhere, and most educated Chinese can speak what we call Mandarin, the language of Peking and the language of officials. In modern

Communist China, Mandarin is now known as National Speech, and it is hoped that this will become the universal language. Meanwhile, however, the dialects in some parts of the country are so different that they are really different spoken languages, and those who speak them cannot understand one another. This means that the same Chinese character, meaning the same thing, may be pronounced quite differently and also be romanized differently. Chiang Kai-shek, for instance, is the southern pronunciation of the name; in the north it is pronounced and sometimes written as Chiang Chieh-shih. The name which is pronounced Wu in Mandarin, and therefore generally romanized as Wu, in the southern dialect would be Ng.

Some generally accepted system of romanization is therefore essential. In English the Wade romanization of Chinese sounds is the most generally used, and still one of the best. Wade, however, apparently heard the b, g, j and d sounds as p, k, ch and t, and wrote them that way. He therefore had to write the actual sounds p, k, ch and t with an aspirate: p', k', ch' and t'. In Wade romanization the city we call Peking is written Pei-ching, although it is actually pronounced "bey-jing." What is spelled "ch'in" is pronounced "chin," whereas "chin" is pronounced "gin." "T'ung" is pronounced "tung"; "tung" is "dooung."

The Chinese, Japanese and Koreans all generally place the surname before the given name. Mao is the surname and Tze-tung the given name of Chairman Mao. In Japan, Tokugawa was the family name of the Shogun Tokugawa Ieyasu.

The names of Chinese emperors can be especially confusing. On succeeding to the throne they changed their personal names for a reign name. During the earlier dynasties—that is, before the Mongol conquest—they usually adopted several different year-names or reign names during their lifetimes, names which often commemorated some special occasion or a magical number, and which they might use for only a few months or for many years. The founder of the Ming Dynasty, Chu Yüan-chang, fortunately set a new style by adopting his original reign name, Hung Wu, for the whole of his reign. He should correctly be referred to as the Hung Wu Emperor, not as Emperor Hung Wu; Ch'ien Lung should be the Ch'ien Lung Emperor, and so forth, but most writers now use the easier if slightly inaccurate form of address. Similarly in Japan, the Emperor who assumed power in 1868 is called Emperor Meiji, although Meiji was actually the name of his reign.

Where proper names are well known in the West, I have used the familiar form, regardless of system; Nanking and Peking instead of Nan-ching and Pei-ching; Taiping rather than T'ai-p'ing, Tartar instead of Tatar. Otherwise I have followed the Wade romanization, falling back on Herrmann's *Historical Atlas of China* for some place names.

Anachronisms are almost inevitable. The lands north and northeast of China may be referred to as Mongolia and Manchuria before those names actually came into being. I have sometimes called Korea, Korea, even at a time when it would more correctly be Koryŏ or Chosen. Not to do so in these cases would, I think, only add to the confusion of unfamiliar names. For the same reason, there may be reference to the policies of China, or the Chinese government, during the Ch'ing Dynasty, at a time when the rulers of China were actually Manchus.

Prologue

THE END OF THE FOURTEENTH CENTURY saw great changes in China, Japan and Korea alike. In all three countries new rulers and new dynasties were coming into power, and all three nations were moving forward into a period of comparative stability and brilliant artistic achievement.

In Japan, the Kamakura Shogunate, which had ruled the country for over two hundred years, had been overthrown by rival feudal lords, and there were years of chaos and confusion before a new Shogunate, the Ashikaga, finally established their supremacy in 1392 (although they preferred to date their assumption of power from 1336). It was also in 1392 that the Yi Dynasty, which was to prove one of the longest-lasting in the entire history of the Orient, was founded in Korea.

In China, the Ming Dynasty, which was to hold the throne until the mid-seventeenth century, had been established somewhat earlier, in 1368. By the turn of the century, the Mings were in firm control of all China; their ships were sailing as far as Africa, and their great capital at Peking was already under construction.

This change of pattern and of rulers in China, Korea and Japan was by no means coincidental. As we shall see, the upheavals, the transformations and the rebirth of the three countries at this time were the result of the vacuum left behind in Asia by the downfall of the great Mongol empire. East Asia during the thirteenth and early fourteenth centuries had been dominated by the Mongols. Even in countries such as Japan, which maintained their independence, the government, the economy and the everyday life of the people were influenced by the very existence of this vast and seemingly all-powerful empire. The Mongol conquests and the century of Mongol rule throughout Asia were a break in the history of that area, an interval between acts, after which the curtain was to rise on a different scene.

This new act in the long history of China, Japan and Korea which began in the fourteenth century was, however, to a great extent a deliberate attempt to repeat the earlier stages of that history. People wanted to return to the great days of Han and T'ang in China, the Heian period in Japan, of Silla and Koryŏ in Korea. They wanted to forget the alien people who had interrupted the continuity of their individual cultures and forced them to recognize a foreign overlord. While moving inevitably into the future, they wanted to look back, to build on ancient glories and to recover the inspiration of their earlier civilizations.

To appreciate this, we should take a quick glance back to the origins of Oriental civilization. Although new discoveries are constantly pushing back the frontiers of time, the earliest civilization of which traces remain would seem to have been born in China, along the Yellow River basin, somewhere between 3000 and 2000 B.C. Because of the impassable mountain ranges which cut it off from the west, the inhospitable deserts of the north and northwest, and the oceans of the south and southeast, this Chinese civilization developed independently. Some outside influences may have filtered across Central Asia, but on the whole, China's language, her culture, her form of government and society, her religions—with the exception of Buddhism, which came from India—were very much her own.

The Shang-Yin Dynasty (*ca.* 1523-1027 B.C.) already had a highly developed civilization, and Shang bronzes are among the finest ever cast anywhere in the world, while the succeeding Chou Dynasty (1027-255 B.C.) was the time of the great Chinese philosophers. It was during the latter half of the Chou Dynasty that Lao Tzu and Confucius founded the two very different schools of religion and philosophy which were to influence the entire history of Asia.

Towards the end of the Chou Dynasty, China had broken up into a number of independent or semi-independent States. During the third century B.C., however, the State of Ch'in conquered or absorbed the other States, and in 221 B.C. the whole of China was united under Ch'in Shih Huang Ti, or the First Universal Emperor. It was he who built the Great Wall to mark the northern frontiers of China.

The Ch'in Dynasty was soon succeeded by the Han (206 B.C.-220 A.D.) and, after a long interval when north and south were split into separate kingdoms, by the T'ang (618-907). These were great epochs in Chinese history. The Han empire was comparable to that of Rome, its contemporary. The T'ang empire far eclipsed that of any European power of the time, and was renowned not only for its conquests but for its art, its magnificent capital at Ch'ang-an and its religious tolerance. The T'ang was the golden age of poetry and painting, as the Han had been of sculpture.

Meanwhile, Chinese civilization had gradually penetrated Korea. During the Han Dynasty, Chinese forces actually occupied the northern part of the country and established a colony which they maintained until 313 A.D. The Koreans adopted the Chinese written language, Chinese systems of administration, and Buddhism and Confucianism in turn. Yet they had a style of their own; during the Three Kingdoms period (fourth to seventh centuries A.D.) and the succeeding Kingdom of Silla (668-935) they established a definitely Korean pattern of life and art which exists to this day.

Chinese writing, art, Buddhism and other cultural influences first reached Japan by way of Korea, then directly, from about the fifth and sixth centuries A.D. Although prehistoric settlements in Japan can be traced back through the second millennium B.C., Japanese civilization developed late. This was, no doubt, partly because of her isolated position. Even the south coast of Korea, which is Japan's nearest neighbor, is over a hundred miles away by sea; moreover, the early centers of Korean civilization were not in the south but far in the northwest, near the borders of China.

Japan, first imitating everything Chinese, then developing her own culture, rapidly made up for lost time. Already in the Heian period (794-1185) Japanese art, architecture, bronze and lacquer work were superb. Heian culture seems almost decadent for so young a country. While much of the land remained primitive and undeveloped, and its people poor, the noblemen of the Heian capital at Kyoto spent their leisure time composing impromptu poetry, watching polo and holding competitions to choose the most beautiful garden, the sweetest-singing bird or the most fragrant perfume.

This delightful but artificial world came to an end when a long-standing feud between two great families ended in the triumph of one of these, which then extended its control over the entire country. Their leader, with the title of Shogun, established his headquarters at Kamakura, where his successors continued to rule until 1336. The official capital remained at Kyoto, but the Emperor there no longer exercised any real power.

In China, meanwhile, the Sung Dynasty had come to the throne in 960, ending a half-century of civil war which followed the downfall of the T'ang. The scattered nomad tribes north of the Great Wall, whom the Chinese called the barbarians, were, however, now united under strong leadership, and they occupied parts of north China. First the Khitan, and then the Juchen Tartars established kingdoms which straddled the Great Wall, making Peking their capital, so that the Sung Dynasty never ruled the whole of China.

Artistically, the Sungs were the equal of the earlier great dynasties. More important, their ideals of government, of a stable, harmonious society led by virtuous emperors under the eternal guidance of Confucius and the Classics, were as fundamental to the regime as they had been for over a thousand years, and as they were to be for succeeding dynasties. It was because of these ideals, first adopted during the Han Dynasty, that the Chinese of any dynasty were proud to call themselves Men of Han.

One must stress the importance of the Chinese belief that the ideal society had already been achieved. There had been a Golden Age. Whatever was wrong in the present, whatever the current problems might be, it was because something had disturbed the harmony and stability which had existed in the past. The aim was always to get back to the original ideal. Progress was not a concept which applied at all. It is no coincidence that the Chinese see, or saw, time as going downward and backward instead of forward and upward, as the West does.

Early in the thirteenth century, the brilliant culture of the Sung Dynasty, the undisturbed peace of Korea under the Kings of Koryŏ (935-1392), and the remarkable growth of a unified Japan under the Kamakura Shogunate, were all violently interrupted by the Mongol conquests.

Seven hundred years later, we can still feel something of the terror inspired by the wild, apparently invincible Mongol hordes who overran Asia. Under Genghiz Khan and his successors, they swept from Mongolia to Moscow and the borders of Hungary, through Persia and into Arabia, to the mountain passes north of India, through China and Korea, until their empire reached from the Pacific Ocean to the Persian Gulf and the Black Sea.

Sung China was not easily conquered. Genghiz Khan died in 1227, and it was only in 1279 that his grandson, Kublai, completed the conquest of the south and proclaimed the Yüan, or Mongol, Dynasty in China proper. Korea had been occupied meanwhile; in 1274 and again in 1281 the Mongols invaded Japan, twice establishing a beachhead, and twice being driven off only because of fierce storms; Mongol armies moved into Vietnam where they occupied Hanoi, and their fleets ranged as far as Burma, the Malay Peninsula and Indonesia.

The Mongols were savage fighters, destroying whatever stood in their way. The Mongol empire, however, united a great part of the civilized world under a single ruler and a single law, bringing East and West into peaceful contact with each other. For the first and almost only time, the caravan routes of Central Asia were open to all, and anyone who had the approval of the Great Khan could cross them without fear or hindrance. Traders like Marco Polo and his uncles, Christian missionaries like Friar John of Plano Carpini and Friar William of Rubruck, ambassadors from Europe and merchants from Arabia were all welcome at the court of the Great Khan. The Mongols employed many foreigners in their government and civil service, regardless of their nationality or religion.

This century of peace under the Mongol rulers may cause us to underestimate the lasting effects of the Mongol conquests. The terror remained. When the Mongols were driven out of China, the native dynasty which succeeded them was determined at all costs to prevent any new invasion. Within half a century, its rulers had withdrawn behind the Great Wall, closing both land and sea routes to the West and entering into an isolation which they tried to preserve even in the nineteenth and twentieth centuries—an isolation which partially explains their reaction to the later "barbarians" who came by sea.

In Japan, although the Mongol invasions failed, they had shown how vulnerable the islands were. For years thereafter, the Japanese lived in fear of a third invasion, and the cost of maintaining their defenses went far to ruin the country's economy and hasten the breakdown of the central government. Japan, too, may have been remembering those Mongol invaders when she closed her ports to the Europeans in the seventeenth century, withdrawing into an isolation more rigid and absolute than that of China.

Korea had been devastated by Mongol occupation. She recovered, enjoying a century or more of peace before invasions came from another quarter, but she never forgot her suffering under the Mongols. [In Vietnam, even now, the Mongols of seven centuries ago are remembered with bitter hatred, and the leaders who resisted them are national heroes.]

Thus as we come to the beginning of the fifteenth century, we should not forget the shadow which lay across East Asia at that time—the fear that the barbarians would return. We know now that the Mongol power was broken, and would ebb away as quickly as it had risen, but the peoples of China, Japan, Korea and their neighbors could not know that, and they were left on the defensive. The past nightmare colored their thoughts for years to come.

I. *Foundation of the Ming Dynasty*

THE YŪAN DYNASTY in China, founded by the Mongols in 1279, had been only a part of the great Mongol empire which stretched unbroken from the Pacific Ocean to the Persian Gulf. The dynasty itself was comparatively short lived, holding the throne for less than a century. Its influence on Chinese history and on the relations between East and West was, however, long lasting. The Chinese hatred and contempt for their barbarian rulers spread over into a hatred and suspicion of all foreigners which has lasted to the present day. On the other hand, the glowing accounts of Chinese civilization which were brought back to Europe by Marco Polo and other travelers of that time caused a sensation. Marco Polo's stories of the fabulous

riches to be found in the land he called Cathay were to inspire
Western travelers, merchant-adventurers and Christian missionaries alike for centuries to come.

The years before the collapse of the Yüan Dynasty followed
a pattern common to the last years of other dynasties. There
were natural disasters; scarcely a year passed without drought,
flood or famine in some part of the country. To make up for
the lost crops, taxes were raised just when people were least
able to meet them. The government, short of money, issued
more and more paper currency, until the currency was worth-
less, and men would only barter what they had for what they
needed, not for cash. The central government in Peking gradually lost control over the country; the Mongol leaders fought
and squabbled among themselves, while local rebellions and
even civil war raged in the provinces.

From the middle of the fourteenth century, it thus became
clear that the Mongols must have lost the Mandate of Heaven.
The Chinese believed that their Emperor, called Son of Heaven,
ruled by divine authority, but they also believed that this authority, or mandate, could be withdrawn and transferred to another
man, even to the humblest subject of the Emperor. Whoever
received it had not only the right to rebel and take the throne
for himself, but a positive duty to do so. If the rebellion succeeded and he established a new dynasty, this was proof enough
that he had been given the Mandate of Heaven.

As Mongol authority weakened throughout the country, several Chinese leaders, one of whom was a descendant of the Sung
Emperor deposed by the Mongols less than a century before,
laid claim to the Mandate. The powerful Buddhist Secret Societies, which had sworn to overthrow the Mongol Dynasty,

gave their support to one or another of these rebellious princes. Yet the man who did eventually drive out the Mongols and found a new dynasty was a character so unlikely that his success seemed to confirm the theory that the Son of Heaven was, in fact, chosen by Heaven.

In spite of flattering portraits painted after he came to the throne, Chu Yüan-chang was ugly, with large ears and a nose like a snout. (He was later nicknamed the Pig Emperor, but this was also a play on words; the "chu" of Chu Yüan-chang means "vermilion" but a similar-sounding "chu" means "pig.") He was born about 1328, of poor parents, and was sent out to work as soon as he was old enough to earn a few coppers by herding cattle. He was only sixteen when both his parents starved to death during a local famine. He buried them wrapped in straw, since he had no money for even the cheapest coffin, and then he sought shelter in a nearby Buddhist monastery. The monks themselves were poor, and food was scarce, but they did provide some education, and there Chu Yüan-chang learned to read and write—an ability by no means common among people of his class at that time.

A few years later, the monastery was burned to the ground by revolutionaries who suspected that Mongol spies were in hiding there. The monks fled for their lives, but Chu Yüan-chang, a rebel at heart, escaped and joined the revolutionaries. He soon rose to take command of their forces, displaying a quite remarkable combination of military genius, patience and statesmanship. He then went on to defeat his more powerful rivals in the field one by one, while at the same time building up an enthusiastic following among the common people. In 1356 he occupied Nanking, a city on the Yangtze River strategically placed to control central and south China, and there he established a strong civil as well as military government.

In 1368 Chu Yüan-chang's armies, with the support of the White Lotus Secret Society, staged a surprise attack on the Mongol capital at Khanbaligh (Peking) which succeeded beyond all expectation. The Mongol Emperor fled overnight, and the hated dynasty was at an end. Meanwhile, Chinese families throughout the country who had had Mongol soldiers billeted upon them rose at a given signal and massacred their unwelcome guests. The order for the massacre had been hidden inside Loaves of the Moon, round cakes, stuffed with spices and sweets, which are often exchanged among friends on the so-called Moon's Birthday, the fifteenth day of the eighth month, and which could therefore be sent freely from house to house under the very eyes of the Mongol soldiery.

Chu Yüan-chang called his new dynasty Ming, meaning simply, Brilliant. He took the reign-name of Hung Wu, or Great Warrior, for himself, and he kept his capital at Nanking. At the same time, he sent his fourth son, Chu Ti, to be Regent in Peking and to carry on the fight against the Mongols in the north.

The first years of the Ming Dynasty were troubled ones. The Mongols still held much of north China, and their armies were a constant threat to the newly established dynasty. It was 1371 before they finally retreated beyond the Great Wall, that ancient barrier which divides China from the northern lands. In the south, it was 1382 before the whole of China had been reconquered, and the Middle Kingdom was once again united within her traditional boundaries.

During this time, the armed forces of the Ming pushed their conquests far beyond the Great Wall, and it seemed as though this might be the beginning of a new Chinese empire in Central Asia, in the tradition of the Han and T'ang empires. Hung Wu and his successors, however, were not empire builders. They were content to accept the Wall as their northern boundary, as long as there was no single great power north of the Wall which threatened their own position, and they were very skillful in playing one nomad tribe off against another to prevent the growth of such a power.

Hung Wu ruled from 1368 to 1398, and in those thirty years he set the pattern of government and society which was followed throughout the Ming Dynasty. It was, above all, to be Chinese, avoiding all foreign influence. The ancient ideals of China, the continuity and stability so rudely interrupted by the

Mongols, must be restored. The Mings deliberately modeled themselves on the past, turning to the T'ang and Sung Dynasties for inspiration. At one time, men were even encouraged to dress in the style of T'ang times—the kimono-like gown, girdled at the waist, with long, wide sleeves and voluminous folds around the feet.

Society was governed by Confucian rules of conduct, which stressed moderation and harmony in all things. According to Confucius, if every man behaved correctly to every other man, observing the five important relationships—those between husband and wife, father and son, elder brother and younger brother, ruler and subject, friend and friend—the result would be an ideal government and a contented people. His principles had been variously interpreted through the centuries, especially by the great scholar Chu Hsi in the twelfth century, but they remained a code of morals, law and individual behavior rather than a religion. Such a code was well suited to the early Ming emperors, anxious as they were to establish a stable, conservative government, and to prevent either Buddhism or Taoism from exercising too much influence in the country.

Buddhism, Taoism and Confucianism had existed side by side in China for centuries. They were not mutually exclusive. Taoism was an otherworldly religion, mystical, opposed to all material progress, and summed up in the saying attributed to Lao Tzu—"Do nothing, and all things will be done." Confucianism, as we have seen, was a way of life, little concerned with a man's soul and not at all with any future existence. Buddhism, which reached China from India about the first or second century A.D., filled a gap between these two. Although Buddha himself had preached a religion as unworldly and mystical as Taoism, Buddhism as practiced in China had its temples, its sacred books, incense, music and colorful ceremonies; all this, as well as its promise of a future life, appealed strongly to the people, and it rapidly became the most popular of the three religions.

In his efforts to weaken the influence of Buddhism, Hung Wu also outlawed the Buddhist Secret Societies which had done so much to destroy the Mongols and bring the Ming Dynasty to power. Secret Societies were useful to a rebel but dangerous to a ruler.

In previous dynasties the Chief Minister had been a person of importance, acting independently in some matters. Now Hung Wu abolished this post altogether and ruled through a number of Grand Secretaries, who could only advise, all decisions being in the hand of the Emperor himself. This concentration of power worked well under a strong ruler. When, however, as would inevitably happen, the Emperor was weak, incompetent or both, no one else could exercise authority in his name. Good local government might keep things running for a time, but without a strong Son of Heaven in control, the system must break down.

Great man though he was, Hung Wu in later life grew moody, suspicious and cruel. It may have been partly because of the poverty and tragedies of his early life that now, as Son of Heaven, he believed himself surrounded by enemies. He turned against his own followers, even some of his most loyal comrades-in-arms, and many innocent men were tortured or executed for treason. He turned against his own family, especially after the death of his eldest son, and he became increasingly suspicious of Chu Ti, now called the Prince of Yen, whom he had sent to rule Peking.

In this case his suspicions were well founded. The Prince of Yen, who was as able and ambitious as his father, had probably made up his mind from an early age to become Emperor in his turn. When Hung Wu had sent him, with a comparatively small force, to take control of a large area between Nanking and Peking, his success had been so spectacular that for years afterwards people spoke of the land as having been swept clean by the broom of Prince Yen. Once established in Peking, he consolidated his position there and bided his time.

Hung Wu named the son of his eldest son as his heir. This young prince, however, was no match for Prince Yen; the latter rebelled within a year of his father's death, claiming the inheritance for himself, and marched south from Peking

33

toward the capital to assert his supposed rights. He met with strong opposition from the supporters of the rightful heir, fighting not so much for the prince himself, as for the legitimacy of the succession in the new dynasty. There were three years of bitter civil war before Prince Yen's victorious armies occupied Nanking.

During this occupation the young Emperor disappeared and was never seen again. His disappearance was to haunt the Prince of Yen as long as he lived, for it seemed likely that he had escaped, possibly to another country; more than one pretender later claimed to be the lost heir and won support from the loyalists.

Prince Yen became Emperor under the reign-name of Yung Lo. It is a famous name, one of the most famous in Chinese history. He had proved himself a brilliant, if ruthless general; he was now to prove himself a statesman, a patron of literature and, above all, a builder. Perhaps his greatest monument is the city of Peking (Pei-ching, or Northern Capital) itself.

Yung Lo moved the capital to Peking in 1421. He undoubtedly had personal reasons for doing so, feeling that Nanking was haunted by the spirit of his father Hung Wu, and by the nephew he had deposed. But he was also well aware of the strategic importance of the north. It is significant that, although there were times when China was divided into two independent kingdoms, north and south, it was very rare for a united China to be ruled from the southern capital. It was only during the first thirty years of the Ming Dynasty, and under the Kuomintang in the twentieth century—a time when China was by no means united or at peace—that Nanking was the capital of all China.

Ancient cities had stood on the site of Peking. The capital of the State of Yen was here from about 723 to 221 B.C., and an old name for the capital is Yenching—or the Swallow Capital—since yen means a swallow. Although both the State of Yen and its capital city were destroyed by Ch'in Shih Huang Ti when he conquered the last of the Warring States in 221 B.C., other cities undoubtedly existed on or near the same site throughout history.

In the tenth century, the Khitans, of the Liao Dynasty, built their capital here and called it, confusingly enough, Nanking, or Southern Capital, because they still kept their old capital further north. The Juchen, who overthrew the Khitans in 1135 and founded the Chin (not to be confused with Ch'in) Dynasty, rebuilt and enlarged the same city, adding to the confusion of names by calling it Chung-tu, or Central Capital. Their city was destroyed by the Mongols in 1215 after a long and bloody siege, but Kublai Khan later built his own capital on almost the same site; it was this city which became known to the West through the descriptions of Marco Polo, as Cambaluc or Khanbaligh, the City of the Great Khan.

Yung Lo now reconstructed the old city of Kublai Khan. There was nothing novel about its ground plan, nor about the location of its palaces, towers and temples. Every Chinese capital from the earliest times had been laid out along the same lines, according to certain definite religious and symbolic principles. These were concerned with Feng Shui, or Wind-Water, the art of harmonizing any work of man—especially houses and tombs, the homes of the living and the dead—with the forces of nature. Everything in nature had its influence for good or bad; the points of the compass, the sun and the moon, the location of hills and of lakes, the direction of the prevailing winds and many other factors must always be taken into account.

Chinese architecture, moreover, from that of the Emperor's palace to that of the merchant or simple farmer, generally followed a fixed pattern. It was a style influenced by the form of Chinese society, and especially by their strong family ties. A series of courtyards would be grouped within a walled enclosure, so that different members or groups of the same family occupied different courtyards, yet all formed part of the same compound. The buildings were only one or two stories high, and as the family increased in size or grew more prosperous,

35

YÜAN MING YÜAN
(Old Summer Palace)

SUMMER PALACE

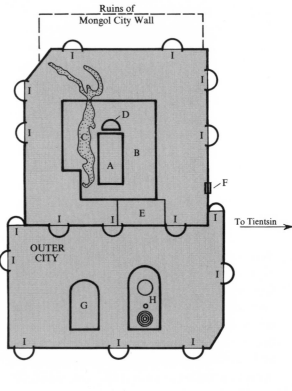

Ruins of
Mongol City Wall

To Tientsin

OUTER
CITY

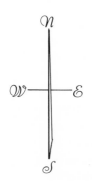

$\mathcal{N}$

$\mathcal{W}$———$\mathcal{E}$

$\mathcal{S}$

A – Forbidden City   F – Observatory

B – Imperial City   G – Temple of Agriculture

C – Lakes   H – Temples and Altar
                 of Heaven

D – Coal Hill

E – Legation Quarter   I – Gates in the City Wall

PEKING

extra courtyards would be added on, so that a town or city grew outward, rather than upward. Even the magnificent imperial palaces of Peking were only one or at most two storied.

The greatness of Yung Lo's vision was in his feeling for space. The Forbidden City, where the Emperor lived, is on a scale that still takes one's breath away. Its great throne rooms, with sweeping roofs of golden-yellow tile and scarlet pillars, stand upon marble platforms, approached by marble steps and carved marble ramps. They are surrounded by huge, paved courtyards where thousands of courtiers, standard-bearers and sometimes even an escort of elephants could assemble on ceremonial occasions.

The Forbidden City was about two miles in circumference, enclosed within high, rose-colored walls and surrounded by a moat. Outside this was the Imperial City, five miles in circumference and also walled, where the nobles lived. This in turn was enclosed by the main, walled city, roughly four miles square, with nine double gates in the wall, each of these a small fortress in itself. Gate towers rose above every gate to a height of ninety-nine feet; this was so that good spirits, which are believed to fly a hundred feet above the ground, could enter the city, while the evil spirits, flying lower, would be shut out. In the sixteenth century an outer city, five miles by two, was added along the south side of the capital, and this was also walled, with gates and gate towers.

Before Yung Lo's time, the city walls had been of beaten mud. Now they were faced with brick, with an inner core of rubble and earth, and they were strengthened at regular intervals with wide buttresses. The walls were forty feet high, thirty feet wide at the top and some sixty feet wide at the base. A flat, paved avenue ran along the top, protected by a high parapet; this provided a sheltered and easily defended rampart which completely encircled the city, and which, with the fortified gate towers, made it almost impregnable to siege. When the city fell, as it did in 1644, it was through treason; the gates were sold, not captured.

It was a city of temples, the Temple of Confucius, the

The Altar of Heaven, Peking. PHOTOGRAPH BY HEDDA MORRISON

Temple of the Ancestors and many others. A Bell Tower and a Drum Tower sounded the watches of the day and night. In the southern city stood the Temple and the Altar of Heaven —unique not only because of their beauty but because they symbolized the divine nature of the Son of Heaven. The prosperity, even the life, of the country and its people were believed to depend upon the annual ceremonies which took place there at the time of the winter solstice, and only the Emperor himself could perform these ceremonies.

What is usually called the Temple of Heaven, includes a number of buildings, surrounded by parkland. The most conspicuous of these is the Hall of Annual Prayers, which is a circular building ninety feet high, standing on a triple terrace of white marble, and crowned with a round, three-storied roof of brilliant blue tile. A marble avenue raised above the ground runs south from this to a smaller circular temple with a single blue roof, where the Emperor used to burn incense and prostrate himself before the sacred tablets on the eve of the winter solstice.

Far more important than either of these buildings, however, was the Altar of Heaven. Set in a broad square south of the two temples, the Altar consists of three round terraces of white marble, one upon another, diminishing in size, each approached by flights of nine steps which are oriented to the four points of the compass. It was so designed that when the Emperor knelt on the center stone of the highest terrace to offer prayers to Heaven he was invisible to the rest of the world. He himself could see only the sky above him and the stones on which he knelt.

It was not surprising if the Emperor, having been escorted with great pomp and ceremony from his, literally, Forbidden

City through gates which were opened for no other man, and kneeling on that Altar alone under the sky, believed himself to be, in fact, the Son of Heaven. Surrounded by ritual, with constant emphasis on his unique position, he had no reason to doubt that the entire world revolved around his majesty, and that he was the divinely appointed ruler of countries whose names he had not even heard.

Thus the whole character of imperial China, including its foreign policy, was influenced by the design of Peking and its Altar of Heaven. Much later, in the eighteenth and nineteenth centuries, China's unwavering conviction that the entire world, All under Heaven, was subject to the Son of Heaven was to play a considerable part in her relations with foreign countries.

This conviction may seem absurd to the Western reader, and by the nineteenth century it certainly bore no relation to the facts. But at the time of Yung Lo, the time when Peking was built, the Chinese had every reason to consider themselves superior men, preeminent in ordered government, culture, technical achievements and military strength. There was no remotely comparable power in the world. The Arab empire was disintegrating, and the Ottoman empire was not yet fully grown; Central Asia and India after the death of Tamurlane were breaking up into petty states and kingdoms; and Europe, although Portuguese and Spanish explorers were beginning the voyages which were soon to carry them around the world, was politically in turmoil. France and England had been intermittently at war for nearly a hundred years, while Spain was still fighting to drive out the last of the Moorish invaders. The Holy Roman Empire was struggling with overpowerful princes, the Papacy was just recovering from its exile in Avignon, and Italy, in spite of the artistic glory of the Renaissance, was split up into small city-states.

China's isolation during the Ming Dynasty, and her consequent ignorance of foreign countries, undoubtedly contributed to the myth of the Emperor's control over the peoples of the earth. But even if Yung Lo and his successors had known a great deal more about the rest of the world than they did, it would only have confirmed their belief in their own superiority.

2. The Brilliant

Dynasty

IN SPITE OF her long coast line, China is essentially a land power. The Chinese are not usually thought of as pioneers in naviagtion, nor in ship-building. Yet there was a time when Chinese ships were larger, more seaworthy and regularly traveled greater distances than those of any other country. Before Prince Henry the Navigator of Portugal had explored the west coast of Africa in the mid-fifteenth century, and long before the age of the great European navigators, before Bartholomew Diaz rounded the Cape of Good Hope in 1488, or Vasco da Gama sailed to India in 1498, Chinese ships were not only masters of the China Sea and the Indian Ocean but were sailing along the east coast of Africa.

The Chinese turned their attention to the sea during the Sung Dynasty (960-1279), when north China was in the hands of the Barbarians and they were therefore cut off from Central Asia and its caravan routes to the West. By the eleventh and twelfth centuries they had become experienced ship-builders and navigators. They had detailed charts of the coasts and islands of Asia, and they were familiar with the shortcut to India through the Straits of Singapore. More important, they understood the nature of the monsoon, those remarkably regular winds which blow from the southwest in summer and the northeast in winter, and timed their voyages accordingly.

The principle of the magnetic compass had been known in China since the third century A.D. Such a compass, pointing south, was apparently in regular use on Chinese ships by 1119, well before European navigators adopted the idea from the Arabs.

Chinese sea power was at its height early in the Ming Dynasty, under Yung Lo. Seven great fleets set sail from South China ports between 1405 and 1433, and although their most profitable trade ventures were in Southeast Asia the first three expeditions all reached India, while other ships sailed on to Aden, the Persian Gulf and East Africa. Some fleets included as many as sixty-three vessels, and Chinese records claim that the largest of these were over four hundred feet long. This is unlikely, but there seems no doubt that they were much larger than European ships of the time; in 1492, nearly a century later, Columbus' Santa Maria was 128 feet long, including the bowsprit. The larger ships had four decks, comfortable private apartments and sometimes even private toilets. One convoy is said to have carried twenty-seven thousand men, including merchants, clerks, government officials and soldiers. Their objectives were, in theory, peaceful, but the armed forces on board were strong enough to compel cooperation on the part of any government which might be reluctant to receive them. A King of Ceylon who resisted the Chinese mission was deposed by force and taken captive to China.

The leader of these expeditions, Cheng Ho, was a eunuch,

one of the few to have contributed real services to his country; a forceful character and a leader of men whether on land or at sea, he had already played an important part in the civil war which placed Yung Lo upon the throne. Being a native of Yunnan, a province in which the Islamic religion was now well established, he was himself a Moslem, and this probably ensured him a friendly reception in the countries he visited, most of which were either Moslem or under Islamic rule.

At this time, China might well have become the dominant sea power in East Asia and in the world, forestalling the Portuguese, the Dutch and the British. Instead, after the death of Emperor Yung Lo in 1424, and of Admiral Cheng Ho in about 1431, the Chinese deliberately turned away from the sea. The last great naval expedition to the west took place in 1433, and thereafter such expeditions were not only discouraged but officially prohibited. "Not an inch of plank," the Emperor said, should go down to the sea. An exception was made for small ships needed to defend the Chinese coast from pirates, but such ships were forbidden to leave the coastal waters; Chinese subjects were also forbidden to travel abroad.

Why was this? One reason was undoubtedly that the great sea voyages had been inspired by Cheng Ho and supported by Emperor Yung Lo for reasons of his own. Yung Lo was an adventurer at heart; moreover, during the early years of the Ming Dynasty it was important to him that the existence of the new dynasty, and his own position as ruler of the Middle Kingdom, should become widely known abroad. It helped to establish the legitimacy of his reign in the eyes of his own people when the kings and emperors of foreign countries sent tribute to him, acknowledging him as the Son of Heaven. Such considerations were of far less importance to his successors.

Another reason for putting an end to the voyages of the Jewel Ships, as they were called, was their expense. The goods they brought back to China were luxuries and curiosities—amusements for the imperial court—not the staples of trade. They carried tribute of exotic birds and animals, ostriches, lions, zebras and giraffes. (The "Auspicious Giraffes" were especially popular because they were identified with the Chinese Ch'i-lin, a mythical animal said to appear only when the Middle Kingdom was ruled by a sage, although Emperor Yung Lo was apparently not impressed by this. "I am no sage," he told the court, "and that beast is no Ch'i-lin.") Precious stones, coral, amber, spices and rhinoceros horn, added to the cargoes but not to the economy of the country. There was nothing to compare with the trade in spices and silk, and later in tea, that was such a magnet to European traders.

There was, however, a more fundamental reason for China's sudden change of policy. The Ming Dynasty was above all isolationist. Her rulers, with the exception of Yung Lo, wanted no contact with foreigners or foreign countries. They simply were not interested in the possibilities of a colonial or commercial empire overseas.

Their withdrawal coincided with the beginning of Europe's great age of exploration, which was to bring her into every corner of the world. The discoveries of Portuguese and Spanish navigators were opening up the seas, and ships could circumnavigate the globe. China's isolationist attitude, which continued through the Ch'ing as well as the Ming Dynasty, cut her off from all this. It was to have a lasting effect on the history of East Asia.

Within its own limits, the dynasty undoubtedly deserved the name it had adopted for itself: Brilliant. But the policy of isolation also meant that the achievements of the Ming Dynasty were never fully appreciated in the West.

Steady economic growth and a growing population contributed to the high level of prosperity. Cities expanded and

The Auspicious Giraffe. FROM AN EARLY COPY, BELONGING TO MRS. J. J. L. DUYVENDAK, OF A PAINTING DATED 1414

new towns came into being; existing roads, houses, temples and city walls were repaired and reconstructed, and there was a constant increase in new building. It is further proof of Ming isolation that every Ming Emperor without exception restored the Great Wall, that ancient barrier which was originally built some sixteen hundred years earlier to protect China from the outside world. The Wall as it now stands is largely of Ming construction.

The canals connecting north and south China, which had fallen into disrepair, were now also completely rebuilt, enabling grain from the rich, rice-growing areas of the south to be shipped north by river and canal rather than by sea. China is lucky in having a vast network of rivers, which, with connecting canals, reaches far into the heart of the country, and these inland waterways have always been an essential means of transport and communication. Where the waterways did not run, transport often had to depend on footpaths, wide enough only for a man or a wheelbarrow.

The country was divided into fifteen provinces. The entire administration from top to bottom, and from the central government in Peking to the minor provincial bureaucrats, was split into three parallel branches: the civil, the military and the censors. The latter were an important body whose duties far exceeded any narrow definition of censorship such as supervising public morals or suppressing undesirable books. Censors were to be chosen for their honesty and fearlessness, not by rank. They were expected to investigate abuses of power or corruption anywhere in the country, to make sure that officials were honest and efficient, that taxes were collected and granaries kept full. Another important function was to listen to the grievances and complaints of the people.

Ideally, the censors acted as the eyes and ears of the Emperor, reporting directly to him. Even the Son of Heaven was not above their criticism; it was their duty to admonish their ruler if he abused his high position. It was, of course, a brave man who would tell a dissolute Emperor the truth about himself or those close to him, when this meant risking torture and death. There were, nevertheless, censors who did exactly that and died for it, while others played an important part in government reform.

(J. K. Fairbank in *East Asia: the Great Tradition*, makes an interesting comparison with modern times: "Since 1928 China has been governed through the three principal echelons of party, army and government. First Chiang Kai-shek and then Mao Tse-tung have stood at the top of this tripod as indispensable foci of final power, somewhat like emperors of old. . . . The party apparatus, however, running parallel to army and civil administration, seems also to have inherited some of the ancient censorial functions.")

Outside the capital an important part in the country's administration was played by the class often called gentry. These were educated men, usually landowners, who were influential in local society and who formed an aristocracy of their own, not necessarily hereditary. It was they who supported schools and charities, who raised money for repairing local roads and bridges and who gave their own time to keep the machinery of local government running smoothly. They lived by Confucian principles, believing in fixed rules of conduct and an orderly, unchanging society. In a country the size of China, their services were absolutely essential; as long as they remained active and loyal, the provinces could be administered by a comparatively small central bureaucracy.

There was a sharp division between classes, the educated scholar-administrator being considered far superior to any other class. This did not mean, however, that the three lower classes —farmers, artisans, merchants, in that order—were exploited or downtrodden. Although in times of famine and civil war, it was inevitably the poorer people who suffered first and most severely, in the long centuries of peace and stability, they shared in the general prosperity of the country. Because of the importance of the family in Chinese society, they also enjoyed a form of security different from but certainly equal to anything known in the more individualistic society of the West.

The younger and more prosperous members of a family

cared for the elderly, the ill and the unemployed. The family took the place of the insurance benefits, old-age pensions and health insurance of our day. They lived together—grandparents, parents, sons, daughters-in-law, children of all ages—in a single compound, enclosed by a single wall. There were individual units, with the smaller family groups having their own bedrooms and kitchen, but much of the life was communal; the inevitable lack of privacy was made up for by the advantages of mutual responsibility, which protected the weaker members of the clan. It was a very interdependent and stable society. The ceremonies and sacrifices held in honor of one's ancestors meant that the family was also a religious unit.

The family was the strongest influence, but guilds and secret societies also played a part in binding the Chinese people together. Members of different trades, even the beggars and the professional mourners at funerals, had their own guilds, some of which claimed to trace their origins back to the Han if not to the Chou Dynasty. They were in many ways similar to modern trade unions; it was almost impossible to practice a particular art or craft without belonging to the guild of that craft.

The close-knit nature of the family, which was based on Confucian principles, may account for the resilience and stability of Chinese society through the trials and troubles of the centuries. The interaction of the gentry and the family system made the administration of such a huge country by a single government much easier; it also meant that the life of the common man might remain comparatively undisturbed by upheavals in the capital and the central government. The convulsions and civil war which marked a change of dynasties, and the chaos of the late nineteenth and early twentieth centuries, should not make us overlook the unique continuity of Chinese life and the well-being of her people in earlier times.

Almost equally important to this stability was agriculture. Rival emperors might battle for the Mandate of Heaven, but the farmer and the peasant carried on the work of their ancestors and taught their children to follow in their footsteps.

48

China lived by the land. The farmers were a class above the artisans and the traders; every spring the Emperor himself ploughed a symbolic furrow of earth, showing the honor in which agriculture was held, and his representatives throughout the country were supposed to do likewise.

Most of the farms were small, even if they formed a part of larger units, and many farmers owned their own land. The owners of larger estates also generally lived on the land, a part of the gentry who formed the backbone of the country, and even those laborers who did not own land were by no means necessarily serfs. When times were hard, however, and especially in periods when a growing population had outrun resources, the peasants often had to tie themselves to overlords in order to survive, and it was then that they became the victims of oppression and abuse.

Comparisons with the West, especially after the Industrial Revolution, are misleading. It is fashionable nowadays to say that the life of the poorer Chinese before modern times was "nasty, brutish and short." Life for the Chinese peasant, as for his counterpart all over the world, was certainly hard. But within their own frame of society, and given a minimum of good central government, they managed well. They were hardworking, self-respecting and, above all, resourceful. Nothing was wasted, even ashes and mineral-rich soil from canals and rivers were used as fertilizer. Several crops might be grown together on the same field, ripening at different times, but the soil was kept fertile by rotating crops, by digging some crops under before they were ripe in order to provide green manure, by composting and by returning every drop of sewage and manure to the earth. The Chinese diet was also very economical. Little land was wasted on animals; grain and vegetables were consumed directly instead of being fed to cattle to provide meat, while the pigs and chickens which were used for meat lived on scraps or by scavenging. Fish raised in ponds or lakes provided extra protein without needing extra land. (Since the Chinese do not drink milk, and seldom use cheese or butter, there was no dairy farming.)

Heating for houses was equally frugal. Although the Chinese never used under-floor heating, as did the Koreans, most rooms had a *k'ang*, a broad bed of brick or earth with flues running horizontally through it, so that a single small fire would heat the entire bed; this was used not only for sleeping but also during the day, almost as a small, extra, heated room. In cold weather, instead of using fuel to warm an entire house, quilted garments were added, one after another, to the loose-fitting trousers and jacket which were the common dress. (In the north, where winters are extreme, a cold day might be called a two-coat or a three-coat day.)

The new rulers reduced the excessive taxes and labor which the Mongols had demanded, but they still collected two annual fees, a Summer and an Autumn Tax. Men of certain classes were also liable to provide a fixed number of days' work during the year. In the beginning, the burden of taxes was fairly spread, but the system was so complicated that there were endless possibilities of falsifying the records. Many wealthy families avoided taxation altogether, shifting the burden onto the poor. During the sixteenth century, therefore, provincial authorities combined the different demands into a single tax, usually collected in silver, rather than grain. This reform was known as the Combination in one Item (often referred to, by a play on words, as the Single Whip) and it was reasonably successful until the early seventeenth century, when the entire structure of the Ming Dynasty gradually collapsed.

The civil service examinations were all important during the Ming Dynasty, and, indeed, until the twentieth century. These examinations were remarkably successful in bringing the most educated and most talented men in the country into positions of high authority in the government. Their weakness was that they were based almost exclusively on the Confucian Classics as interpreted by Chu Hsi in the twelfth century. It was not what you thought; it was how you expressed it in relation to the Classics that mattered. In the fifteenth century a rigid form of examination paper, known as the Eight-legged Essay because it was divided into eight sections, was introduced, and the result was an even more narrow and orthodox system of learning.

There was a series of qualifying examinations in the country towns, in the principal cities of each prefecture and in the provincial capitals, before the final examinations in Peking. The latter were held every three years. Five or six thousand candidates, already screened by the earlier examinations, would assemble at the Hall of Examinations, where each was assigned to a separate cubicle, five feet square and ten feet high, furnished with a table, a stool and writing materials. They changed their clothes outside the cubicle, lest they try to smuggle in books or notes. Then a different character was written on the door of each cell, and the candidate marked his papers with the same character; the examiners did not know his name or even what province he came from. After each one entered his cell, the door was sealed up and not opened again—not even if, as sometimes happened, a candidate went mad, died or committed suicide —until all the papers had been collected at the end of three days.

Those passing the final examination were qualified for the highest academic degree, which they received at a ceremony before the Emperor in person. It is said that long ago, during the T'ang Dynasty, the most brilliant scholar, by far, was one Chung K'uei, who was unfortunately also very ugly. When he went to receive the golden rose which was the symbol of his success from the hands of the Emperor, the Son of Heaven was so taken aback that he involuntarily dropped the rose and it fell, broken, at Chung K'uei's feet.

Overcome by shame, Chung K'uei fled from the palace and tried to drown himself. At that moment, however, a great sea monster rose out of the water, lifted Chung K'uei upon his back and soared up to heaven. There the scholar, having become immortal, made his home in the constellation of the Great Bear; he is one of the gods of literature and the patron saint of students, and in the old days young men working for the examinations would keep a picture of him hanging above their desks. (Such pictures were often caricatures made out of the characters for the name of the god of literature.)

There could be no question of the brains, ability and perseverance of the officials chosen by this method. When a similar system of civil service examinations was adopted in Japan and Korea, it was restricted to the hereditary upper classes, but in China the examinations were genuinely open to rich and poor alike. (The rich, of course, did have the advantage that it was easier for them to support a son through all the years of study and examinations.) The disadvantage of the system, as we have seen, was that by the time they reached high office their thinking was usually conservative and inflexible.

The scholars were the elite of society. They would grow the nails on their little fingers several inches long, wearing a silver or enameled shield to protect them, thus making clear that they never used their hands for anything except writing or painting. They took little if any exercise—only fishing was considered a truly scholarly occupation—and they deliberately walked with stooped shoulders, lost in thought.

The literary output of the time was enormous. Many of the most famous Chinese novels date from the Ming Dynasty, among them *The Water Margin* (also translated as *All Men are Brothers*), an adventurous tale of a band of brigands during the twelfth century; *The Golden Lotus*, an erotic story which has been much censored at various times; *Journey to the West*, a light-hearted account of a very unorthodox pilgrimage to India (translated by Arthur Waley as *Monkey*); and, the best known and probably earliest of all, *Romance of the Three Kingdoms*, a story of the stirring times after the fall of the Han Dynasty in the third century.

The Chinese theater is said to have been founded in 720 A.D. by a group of players calling themselves Brethren of the Pear

Chung K'uei (a caricature made from the characters for the name of the God of Literature).
A STONE-RUBBING FROM AN OLD TABLET AT SIAN, SHENSI

Garden, but it then consisted mostly of music and poetry, accompanied by stylized gestures. True drama was introduced during the Yüan (Mongol) Dynasty, and most of the best-known plays were written at that time or early in the Ming Dynasty. These are lively and colorful, and although they were staged without scenery or properties this only added to the action; actors had to make clear by their movements when they were mounting an imaginary horse, rowing across a river or climbing an unseen flight of steps.

The most remarkable works of the Ming Dynasty, however, were not the popular novels and plays but the encyclopedias and what are called, for want of a better word, collections. There were books on every conceivable subject—animal, vegetable and mineral; there were textbooks on the manufacture of paper, silk, pottery and different metals, on the production of coal, and other industries. These were in great detail, and many are still valuable today. To take a single example: two writers devoted eighteen years to a study of how to survive during a famine, and produced a manual, published in 1406 and illustrated with woodcuts, describing over four hundred plants which were usually to be found even in times of drought or flood, and which were safe to eat.

Such works were dwarfed by the great encyclopedia of the Emperor Yung Lo. This was compiled over several years by two thousand scholars. It consisted of 11,095 volumes, and was meant to include everything of value that had been written on any subject up to the end of the fourteenth century. It covered science, art, history, administration, religion, literature, geography and so on. Although some volumes were printed from woodblocks, the complete work was too enormous to be printed as a whole. Three manuscript copies were made, which must have been a terrific work in itself, but over the years many volumes have been lost (almost the whole of one original manuscript was destroyed when the Hanlin Academy was burnt by the Boxer rebels in 1900) and only about four hundred still exist.

There were many brilliant Ming painters, among them

The Tomb of Yung Lo. PHOTOGRAPH BY GILLIAN WILSON

scholarly amateurs who painted because they believed that poetry, painting and calligraphy (writing Chinese characters, which is done with a brush, is in itself a form of painting) were essential to man's understanding of nature. There were original, almost impressionist artists. But painting as a whole, and sculpture too, reflected the Ming desire to seek inspiration in the past, and painters did not hesitate to copy and recopy the masters of earlier dynasties. As in the examinations, method and detail were more important than originality.

The porcelain of the Ming Dynasty is probably the finest ever made. Porcelain is an advanced type of pottery, using fine clay fired at very high temperatures. The word, surprisingly, comes from the Italian *porcellana*, or cowrie shell, a shell with a smooth glazed surface, and *porcellana* in turn comes from the

Latin *porcellus*, or, little pig, the shape of the cowrie shell being rather like a pig's back. China is rich in different clays, and the Chinese had been master potters long before the Ming Dynasty, but now they were able to produce porcelain so thin that it was translucent, and so hard that steel would not scratch it.

The purest clay comes from a hill near Ching-te-chen, in Kiangsi Province, south of the Yangtze River, and we still call it kaolin, from *kao-ling*, or the high ridge. The kilns at Ching-te-chen, founded during the Sung Dynasty, were perhaps the most famous in China but many other potteries turned out equally fine ware, far superior to anything which could be produced elsewhere in the world.

In style, Ming porcelain showed the influence of the brief Mongol period. By the end of the Sung Dynasty the design and coloring of vases, bowls and other porcelain vessels had become so refined, so austere and perfect of its own kind, that it really could develop no further along the same lines. The Mongols introduced new shapes and techniques, more flamboyant, even vulgar, and although the Ming artists discarded many of these they were inspired by others, especially by the use of blue and white decoration.

Many colors were used in Ming porcelain, especially after the fifteenth century, but it is the beautiful blue-and-white ware which is most typical of the dynasty. This was partly because the cobalt used for the blue withstood the high temperatures necessary in firing fine porcelain better than other colors. In the early years of the dynasty a local cobalt was used, and the blue was distinctly greyish; later a more vivid blue cobalt was imported from Persia.

The fine porcelains, the paintings and architecture, the novels, the great encyclopedias, as well as the remarkable stability of its society, and the steady increase in its population, all point to the prosperity of the Ming era. Chinese culture and civilization could compare with any in the world, to the advantage of China. Yet it remained virtually unknown to the West.

3. Western Approaches
to China by Sea

CHINA NEVER altogether banned foreigners from her shores, as the Japanese were to do from the seventeenth to the mid-nineteenth centuries. She was not afraid, as the Japanese were, of the effect of foreign ways and foreign inventions upon her ancient culture, or of Christianity opening the way to foreign conquerors; she was too conscious of her own superiority.

The Chinese felt that if other countries wished to share in China's superior culture, they should declare themselves her vassals and send tribute, and as long as they behaved with due respect and humility they would be tolerated. If they wished to have the porcelains and the silks in which China was so rich, they might receive these in exchange for their tribute. This fundamental reaction of the Chinese toward foreigners and foreign trade was to cause much misunderstanding in later years, when the Europeans were thinking of the right to trade on favorable terms as a perfectly reasonable demand to make, whereas China considered any trade with foreigners as a concession on her part.

The nomad tribes north of the Great Wall regularly sent tribute to China and received gifts in return. During the Ming Dynasty, however, the exchange of tribute and gifts had become nothing more than an ordinary business transaction, and one in which the Chinese were generally the losers. In order to maintain the fiction that all merchants bringing goods into China were official embassies paying tribute to the emperor, they had to be treated as guests, housed, fed and entertained. When, in addition, the gifts given them had to be of equal value to their tribute, it is easy to see how expensive the tribute missions were to their hosts, and why the Chinese insisted on limiting their number.

Horses and furs were the usual tribute from the north. In exchange, the nomads received textiles, silk, knives and other weapons and utensils, with occasional luxuries such as musical instruments. From the latter part of the Ming Dynasty, brick-tea was also an important item of Chinese trade with the north. Brick-tea was made from inferior tea leaves pressed into the shape of bricks and therefore easy to transport; its flavor was not very delicate, but it was strong, and since the Mongols often brewed their tea for hours at a time, they may have preferred it that way.

In addition to the overland trade, there was trade with Japan. Relations between the two countries varied, but it was usually the Japanese who took the initiative and sent so-called tribute missions, embassies bearing gifts of gold, lacquer, swords, finely wrought armor and other manufactures at which the Japanese excelled. These all had to be paid for, and eventually the Japanese missions became such a drain on China that they, too, were strictly limited.

Now, however, an entirely new world was to appear at the gates of China. There were several reasons for this. Marco Polo's description of his travels in Cathay, of the great cities and the rivers spanned by marble bridges, the gold and the jewels, the vast imperial palaces, and the luxuries enjoyed even by the common people, had caught the imagination of Europe. Other men were determined to follow in his footsteps.

Marco Polo, however, had traveled at a time when the vast extent and firm government of the Mongol empire made it possible for men to reach China either by land across Central Asia or by sea from the Persian Gulf. The position was now quite different. Central Asia was split into separate states and kingdoms, often at odds with one another, and the overland route to China was extremely hazardous. The Red Sea and the Persian Gulf routes were dominated by Moslem countries, hostile to the Christians. If the Europeans were to travel to and from the Orient, as they were determined to do, it was essential to find an all-sea route from Europe to East Asia which avoided the Moslem states of the Middle East.

It was not the porcelain, the silks, or the gold of China, valuable although these were, which made the West so eager to open up a sea route to the East, and inspired the Portuguese and Spanish expeditions of the fifteenth and sixteenth centuries, and those of the Dutch and British somewhat later. It was the spices of Southeast Asia. It is hard for us to realize how important these spices—pepper, cloves, nutmeg, cinnamon and ginger—were to the West at this time. The food of most Europeans was neither plentiful nor varied. There was no refrigeration except that of a cold winter. Livestock had to be slaughtered in the fall because there was nothing to feed the animals during the winter, and for much of the year the only meat available was dried, stringy and tasteless, if not actually bad. Spices, which made the food palatable, were perhaps the most valuable commodity in the world.

The spices came from India and Southeast Asia, especially from the islands of present-day Indonesia, and they had formerly been transported overland from India. Now that this overland

route was no longer safe, the need for a direct route to the spice islands brought about a new era of navigation. Columbus, Vasco de Gama, Magellan and many others sailed in search of the Indies. Later, even after the discovery of the Americas, the attempt to find a Northwest Passage from the Atlantic to the Pacific Oceans, which was to lead many gallant explorers far into the Arctic, was inspired by the hope of finding a shortcut to the spice islands.

This, of course, was not the only reason for the exploits of European navigators and the sudden expansion and empire-building of the European countries at this time. Knowledge of the world was increasing. Map-makers were better informed, and their charts more accurate, while ship-builders were learning new skills and techniques. Also, there are times in history when, for no obvious reason, there is a sudden explosion of talent and new ideas in a particular field—the artists of the Renaissance; the architecture of England at the time of Christopher Wren; Periclean Athens; the T'ang Dynasty in China, when painters and poets set the standard for a thousand years. The fifteenth and sixteenth centuries were the Age of Exploration.

These European navigators knew well enough where China and the Indies were to be found. It was generally agreed, long before Columbus' time, that the world was round and that the Orient could be reached by traveling east or west. It was a question of distance and of what lay between. Should one sail east, around Africa and by way of the Indian Ocean? Or was there a shorter route west across the Atlantic?

Most of the Portuguese explorers, believing that Africa did not extend far south of the equator and that once they had

"Returning from a Spring Outing," by Tai Chin (ca. 1430), painting, Ming Dynasty. COLLECTION OF THE NATIONAL PALACE MUSEUM, TAIPEI, TAIWAN, REPUBLIC OF CHINA

rounded the desolate Sahara coast, as Prince Henry the Navigator's ships had done, they could sail due east, chose to explore the African route. It was only as they pushed further and further down the coast that they discovered the vast size of the African continent, and the length of the detour they must make to reach India and Southeast Asia by sea.

A different theory, which gained support among the Spanish, was that the most direct route to the Orient was probably by way of the Atlantic Ocean. The calculations by which they arrived at this conclusion overestimated the width of the land mass dividing Europe from China, and underestimated the circumference of the earth. Subtracting the former from the latter, they concluded that China must lie within sailing distance west of Europe; that it was located, in fact, just about where North America is. (Distances by sea, even when known, were often foreshortened in maps because the parchment on which these were drawn was so expensive that it seemed wasteful to leave great empty spaces for the oceans, and this may have unconsciously influenced men's thinking.) It was Columbus' fanatical belief in the nearness of Asia which gave him such faith in the success of his venture, his idea being to sail due west until he struck the mainland of China, and then to turn south to the spice islands which were his main objective.

The discovery of America delayed Spanish exploration of East Asia. Dreaming of a profitable spice trade, they were not at all pleased with their discovery; it was only later that they appreciated the value of the Americas and began to exploit the vast gold and silver deposits of the southern continent. Meanwhile, the Portuguese, sailing around Africa, were the first to land at a Chinese port. They reached Canton in 1514.

Trade was the primary objective of these early Europeans, closely followed by the hope of converting heathen lands to Christianity, but they also hoped to establish friendly relations with the Asian countries, China in particular. The crew of this first ship seem to have found the Chinese, as far as they could understand one another, friendly and helpful. Unfortunately, the captain of a second Portuguese vessel arriving in Canton in

1519 turned his guns upon the city, plundered its shops, carried off Chinese children as slaves and generally behaved so outrageously that in 1522 the Chinese forebade any Portuguese to land anywhere in China. Such incidents only confirmed the Chinese in their belief that the foreigners from overseas—Yang Kuei-tze, or Ocean Devils, as they named them—were truly barbarians.

About 1557, they relented to the extent of allowing the Portuguese to settle at Macao, which has remained Portuguese from that day to this, and to carry on a limited trade from there. The foreigners were useful to the Chinese in several ways. Their guns protected the south coast of China from the now frequent and devastating raids of the so-called Japanese pirates. (There were both Chinese and Japanese among these raiders, and their main base was on the Chinese island of Chusan.) At the same time, the Portuguese carried on a three-cornered trade between Europe, Southeast Asia and China, which was profitable to all. The Chinese were not interested in most European goods, but they, too, were eager to have the spices, ivory and precious woods of the Indies; Portuguese ships carried these to Macao, where they made a good profit, and then bought Chinese silks, porcelains and tea for the western market.

The Spaniards were not far behind. In 1519, Magellan's five ships crossed the Atlantic Ocean, followed the coast of South America, rounded the straits (which now bear his name), into the Pacific Ocean and sailed on across the South Pacific to land on the Philippine Islands. Magellan himself died there, but one of his ships, sailing back to Spain by way of Africa, completed the first circumnavigation of the globe.

By the end of the sixteenth century, the Spanish were firmly established in the Philippines, with their capital at Manila. For a time, until they were driven out by the Dutch, they occupied Formosa. They never succeeded in settling on the Chinese coast, as the Portuguese had done at Macao, but they did build up a profitable trade between Southeast Asia and China on one hand, and Spain, or the Spanish settlements in the Americas, on the other.

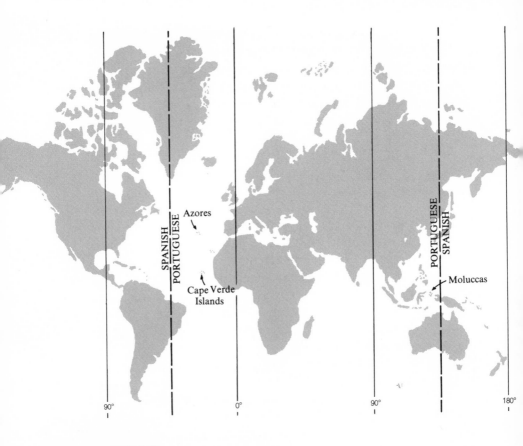

LINE DRAWN BY
THE TREATY OF TORDESILLAS, 1494

Thus the Portuguese coming from the west, and the Spanish from the east, met in the coastal waters of China. As a result, the Portuguese called the Philippines the Eastern Islands, while the Spaniards called them the Western Islands; it all depended where you started from. Meanwhile, the fierce rivalry between Spain and Portugal concerning ownership of the lands newly discovered by their adventurous navigators, had been settled by Pope Alexander VI drawing a straight line on the map from the Arctic to the Antarctic, a hundred leagues west of the Azores and Cape Verde Islands, and awarding all land east of this to Portugal, and all land west of it to Spain. Portugal protested that this was unfair, and a compromise was reached in the Treaty of Tordesillas in 1494 by drawing the line 370 leagues west of the islands. This corresponds roughly with the 50th degree of longitude. It was, however, apparently not clear which of the Cape Verde Islands the 370 leagues should be measured from; when the line was later extended right around the globe, dividing it between the two countries like an apple cut in half, both Spain and Portugal were able to claim the Moluccas, or Spice Islands, which were of great importance to the spice trade.

This rivalry between the European powers did not concern China. Their ships touched only at one or two ports in south China, hundreds of miles away even from the Yangtze River valley, and over a thousand miles from Peking. As far as China was concerned, these foreign merchants who came by sea were no different from the tribes they were accustomed to dealing with on their northern frontiers. The Chinese had no understanding of the distances the strangers had come, nor the technical skill involved in their navigation around the globe, nor of the strength of their arms.

Sweet potatoes, corn, peanuts and tobacco were among the foreign crops which found their way into China during the Ming Dynasty. They did so by circuitous routes, and no one is sure exactly when or where they were first planted. Maize, or Indian corn, for instance, was introduced to Spain from the New World, and it is thought to have been carried by Moorish

pilgrims traveling to Mecca, and from Mecca to China by other pilgrims returning home across Central Asia. It is mentioned by a Chinese writer in 1555; by the seventeenth century it was one of the staple crops of China.

Ever since the great explorer Chang Ch'ien in the second century B.C. had brought grapes, walnuts and alfalfa back from Central Asia, the Chinese had welcomed and experimented with foreign plants. This, together with their ingenuity in making use of every edible native plant, accounts for the remarkably well-balanced diet of the Chinese people, even the poorer classes. Their grains included rice, wheat, millet, barley and oats; they had peas and beans of every kind, including the invaluable soya bean; they used lotus roots and water chestnuts as well as more common root crops; sesamum and rape seeds were pressed for cooking oil. The rape plant and the bamboo served a variety of purposes. The young shoots of both could be eaten, while the dried stems of rape provided useful fuel; bamboo leaves were used for light clothing, and its stalks were strong enough to use in furniture and in building.

Now, the Chinese enthusiastically cultivated not only maize but also the sweet potato, which probably reached China by way of Spanish settlers in the Philippines. Sweet potatoes were especially valuable because they grew well in sandy soil, which was often unsuitable for grain, and their yield per acre was high. The introduction of maize and sweet potatoes alone enabled China to feed many more people, and this was one of the reasons for her steadily increasing population in the seventeenth and eighteenth centuries.

Cotton, although it was not native to China, had long been known there; both raw and manufactured cotton were sent as

Example of early Ming Dynasty sculpture. THE METROPOLITAN MUSEUM OF ART (GIFT OF ROBERT LEHMAN, 1946)

tribute from India, Malaysia and the South Pacific. It was already being planted in China by the twelfth century. Now, however, it was cultivated for the first time on a large scale, and China, during the Ming Dynasty, became an important producer of cotton and cotton cloth, while her own people increasingly wore cotton clothes.

Another commodity imported into China at this time was silver. The Spanish had now discovered the vast riches of the New World, and their silver mines in Mexico and South America supplied the growing demand for this metal in Europe and Asia. China had silver of her own, and silver currency had been used as early as the T'ang Dynasty, but it was only now that it became common. Taxes were collected in silver instead of grain. Some of the large silver coins in use in the Middle Kingdom at this time were actually minted in America, with the curious result that as late as the twentieth century, coins being minted in China, of Chinese silver, were still often called Mexican dollars.

The slow movement of new materials and ideas from West to East was balanced by a similar movement from East to West. While silver was being imported into China, and new crops taking root there, things Chinese were becoming familiar in Europe. Their influence was largely artistic and cultural. It was not until the following dynasty that chinoiserie became a real craze in the West, but even in the time of the Ming Emperors, Chinese designs were being copied in European silks and tapestries, the curve of Chinese roofs was imitated in European pavilions, and there was an insatiable demand for Chinese embroideries, ivory carvings, lacquer, silk, furniture—and, above all, porcelain. Finding the porcelain trade so profitable, China now began producing special export wares, still of fine quality, but designed for foreign markets and suited to the taste of buyers in Persia, Turkey, England and France, rather than China.

In addition to such luxuries and works of art, China and Korea together can probably take credit for the introduction into Europe of one of the most important inventions ever made by man: printing. Printing from woodblocks had been common in China since the ninth or tenth century, and they had experimented with movable type cast in clay as early as the eleventh. The Koreans, however, were apparently the first to use movable metal type; they may well have done so in the thirteenth century, and they certainly printed a book from such type in the year 1409. In an era when so many new ideas were being exchanged between East and West, even though indirectly, it seems extremely likely that Gutenberg's "invention" of movable type in Europe half a century later was based on knowledge of the Chinese and Korean inventions.

4. The Jesuit

Pioneers

Aᴄᴏᴜɴᴄɪʟ of Ephesus in 431 had declared Nestorian Christianity (named for the patriarch, Nestorius) to be a heresy, many Nestorians moved eastward into India, Central Asia and China. There were Nestorian Christian communities in China early in the T'ang Dynasty (618-907) and a large stone tablet describing the arrival of the first Christians was set up in the T'ang capital, Ch'ang-an, in 781. These early communities were, however, almost entirely wiped out by religious persecutions in the ninth century.

Again in the thirteenth and fourteenth centuries, under the Mongols, there were Nestorian Christian settlements in north China and Mongolia. At that time, Roman Catholic missionaries were also active in north China, and in 1295, John of Montecorvino received permission from the Great Khan to build a Catholic church in Khanbaligh, or Peking. Within the next twelve years, Montecorvino was said to have made over six thousand converts.

After the fall of the Mongols, the Ming Dynasty turned against all things foreign. There were religious persecutions. Once again the foreign faith died out, until by the beginning of the sixteenth century no trace of Christianity remained in China.

This was an age of great missionary fervor in the West. European merchants might be drawn to East Asia by the riches to be found there, but men like St. Francis Xavier and Matteo Ricci were driven by their longing to preach the Gospel to the heathen. Pope Alexander's division of the world into Spanish and Portuguese spheres of influence was predicated on the understanding that they would convert the newly discovered pagan lands to Christianity. The first of Vasco da Gama's men to set foot in India is said to have exclaimed, "We come in search of Christians and spices!"

Foremost among the missionaries were the Jesuits, or members of the Society of Jesus, a Roman Catholic religious Order founded by St. Ignatius de Loyola about 1539. Loyola was a soldier, and he saw the Catholic church as being at that time in a state of war against Martin Luther and Protestantism. The Jesuits were carefully chosen, highly trained and dedicated men; they not only took vows of poverty, chastity and obedience, but also a special vow to go anywhere in the world in the service of the Pope. They were the most militant and the most intellectual of the Catholic Orders, and the most active in Asia.

Francis Xavier, one of the founding fathers of the Society of Jesus, reached Japan in 1549. He was well received there and made a surprising number of converts, but he came to the conclusion that he must first convert China to the true faith, whereupon the conversion of Japan would naturally follow. In the light of history, this was not unreasonable. So much of

Japanese culture, including Buddhism, had come from China that if China were to become Christian it would undoubtedly exercise a powerful influence upon Japan.

He had, of course, set himself an impossible task. Foreigners were forbidden to enter the Middle Kingdom. Moreover, a new Law against Heresies introduced in China in 1511 authorized the government to suppress any non-Confucian religion. This was aimed at various irregular sects of Buddhism and Taoism, not at Christianity, but it made it even more unlikely that a foreign religion would be tolerated.

Francis Xavier succeeded in landing on Chinese soil, but only on a small island where there was a Portuguese trading post. He spent the last year of his life there, unable to get permission to enter mainland China, his eyes and his heart set on that great country which he felt must hold the key to the conversion of East Asia. After his death in 1552, other Catholic missionaries carried on his efforts to break into the fortress that was China. They made no progress whatsoever. One or two priests did land in China, defying the regulations, but as soon as it was discovered who they were, they were deported.

The Chinese were obviously not interested in Christianity. It occurred to the Jesuits, however, that they might be interested in other aspects of Western culture; Western science might open a crack in the deliberate, self-satisfied isolation of China where trade and missionary work had failed to do so.

Matteo Ricci, the man who was to put this new theory into practice, was an Italian Jesuit born in 1552, the year that Francis Xavier died. Ricci's zeal was probably as great as that of Xavier, but he was a practical man. He was well versed in the science of his day—mathematics, astronomy, physics and geography; he had a clear mind, a good memory and a gift for languages. His contemporaries described him as a man of great charm, with deep blue eyes and a voice like a bell.

Soon after Ricci came to Macao in 1582, he and a fellow-priest were given permission to live in a town not far from Canton. At first they did not try to convert anyone there to Christianity. They wore the ordinary dress of Buddhist monks, which Ricci later abandoned in favor of the long gown of a Chinese scholar. Speaking, reading and writing Chinese, which he had learned in Macao, Ricci gradually made the acquaintance of Chinese scholars and officials, with whom he discussed mathematics and astronomy. He showed them maps of the world more accurate and more detailed than their own. He became familiar with the Chinese Classics, and when he did discuss Christianity, he tried to show that it need not conflict with the ancient Confucian beliefs and ceremonies. Thus he gradually won the confidence and friendship of the educated Chinese with whom he came in contact.

In 1601, he was allowed to go to Peking, where he was provided with a house and an allowance from the imperial court. His arrival is recorded in the Chinese annals of the time. In fact, he is the only European to be mentioned by name —as Li Ma-tou, the Chinese version of Matteo Ricci—in the dynastic histories of China.

Ricci died in Peking in 1610, after twenty-eight years in China. He had laid the foundation for a long association between the imperial court and the Jesuit fathers, in which the Jesuits' knowledge of such varied subjects as casting cannon and cannonballs, clock-making, astronomy, algebra, Euclidean geometry and the division of the globe by meridians and parallels, proved useful to the Chinese. The astronomy was even more essential than the cannonballs. Soon after they were received at court, the Jesuit astronomers pointed out an error which had been made by Chinese astronomers in predicting the date of an eclipse. When the Jesuits' date for the eclipse proved to be correct, they were not only entrusted with reforming the calendar, they were also put in charge of all astronomical observations, and as a result they became very influential at the Chinese court.

Much of Ricci's work was later to be undone by the Rites Controversy, a conflict within the Catholic Church itself as to how far Christianity was, in fact, compatible with Confucianism. But that was not until late in the seventeenth century. Meanwhile, thanks largely to the prestige of the Jesuit

P. MATTHÆVS RICCIVS MACERAT. of the Society of Iesus, the first propagator of the Christian Religion in the Kingdo of China.

LY PAVLVS GREAT COLAVS OF the Chineses propagator of y Christian Law.

scientists, Christianity made progress. Ricci himself converted at least one imperial prince and two members of the Hanlin Academy, which was the most influential group of literary men in the country. At one time during the seventeenth century, there may have been as many as a quarter of a million Christians in China.

Ricci and other early Jesuits came to China by sea. Strange as it seems now, they were by no means certain that this China was the same Cathay which Marco Polo and other European travelers had visited during the Mongol empire, and whose riches they had so enthusiastically described. Cathay was known to have had Christian churches, including that of John of Montecorvino in Khanbaligh; there had been Christian communities, and at least one Nestorian Christian ruler of a Christian tribe. Yet now, even in Peking, the Jesuits could find no evidence that Christianity had ever been known there.

Cathay and China were both foreign names. The Chinese knew their land as Chung Kuo, the Middle Kingdom, or T'ien Hsia, All under Heaven. In ancient times the Romans and others had called it Seres, or the land from which silk comes. Later travelers approaching China by land, knew it as Khitai, Cathay or some similar name, because of the Khitan Dynasty which ruled north China from the tenth century to the twelfth; in Russian, China is still Khitai. The world of the Great Khan that Marco Polo knew was Cathay, and its capital was Khanbaligh.

China, or Chin, or Sin, on the other hand—a name probably derived from Ch'in Shih Huang Ti, the great emperor of the third century B.C., whose ships traveled as far as the Indian

75

Ocean—was the only name familiar to those who came by sea. Now, in the sixteenth century, European traders and missionaries had undoubtedly reached China. But where was Cathay?

The position was further confused by Moslem merchants who crossed Central Asia into China at about the same time that Matteo Ricci arrived there by sea. Returning to the Middle East, they reported that they had found Christian churches and large Christian congregations still existing in Cathay. The Moslems seem to have spoken in good faith, possibly misled by certain features of Buddhism such as religious music, or statues and paintings of gods and saints, which were entirely alien to Islam but were not unlike the Christian practice. Whatever their motives, their stories seemed to prove that China was not Cathay.

Ricci himself was convinced as soon as he reached Peking that the two countries were one and the same. Geographically, they must be. Many people in Europe, nevertheless, still firmly believed that another country, where Christianity was known and practiced, lay to the north of China proper.

To settle this question the Provincial of the Jesuit Order in India decided to send a small party across Central Asia into the Cathay described by the Moslem merchants, where they would try to make contact with Ricci and his fellow Jesuits in China. The man chosen for this journey was Benedict Goes, a lay brother in the Jesuit order. He traveled disguised as an Armenian Christian merchant, letting his hair grow long and wearing a turban, for this enabled him to visit countries where most other Europeans were unwelcome, and yet did not mean that he had to hide his religious beliefs. When he left Agra in the fall of 1602, he was accompanied by another priest, a Greek merchant and four servants, but all these soon found some good reason for turning back; by the time they reached Kabul, the last stop in the comparatively peaceful lands of the Great Mogul, Goes was alone except for one Armenian servant, Issac.

It would have been folly for the two men to travel alone in those perilous times. After waiting a few months in Kabul, they joined a Persian caravan setting out for Central Asia, and so began a journey of incredible hardship. They crossed the Pamir Mountains, called the Roof of the World, at a height of eighteen thousand feet. Issac barely escaped drowning in one of the great rivers at the base of the mountains; their extra horses were lost in a snowstorm, and Goes himself was thrown down a crevass, from which he was rescued with great difficulty and a sprained leg. They were constantly under attack from armed bandits and constantly in danger of being involved in the local wars and religious feuds of the many petty kingdoms whose borders they had to cross.

The difficulties along this route were so great that most caravans traveled only part of the way, and goods reaching Europe from China, or vice versa, might have changed hands a dozen times. The caravan Goes had been with was disbanded at Yarkand. There the two travelers spent months waiting, resting, asking about the roads ahead, and about possible caravans, meanwhile buying horses, provisions and as much jade as they could afford.

The best jade is found near Yarkand, and caravans bound for Cathay always carried quantities of this precious stone. The Chinese have always had a special feeling and love for jade, not only because of its beauty but because they believed it to possess certain magical powers. Jade was the most valuable gift to present to any Chinese official, and therefore the surest passport into China.

It was almost a year before Goes and Issac found another caravan traveling east along the edge of the vast, barren deserts where no man lived. Then they stopped for days, sometimes weeks, at various staging points along the way; and at one such caravanserai, possibly at Karashahr, they fell in with some Moslem merchants returning from Cathay. In answer to Goes' questions, these men explained quite clearly that Peking, which was the capital of Cathay, had formerly been Khanbaligh. They added that all foreign visitors to the city were accommodated in one large hostelry; they had been staying there, and so had several European priests, who were obviously Jesuits.

Goes now knew beyond all doubt that the Cathay which

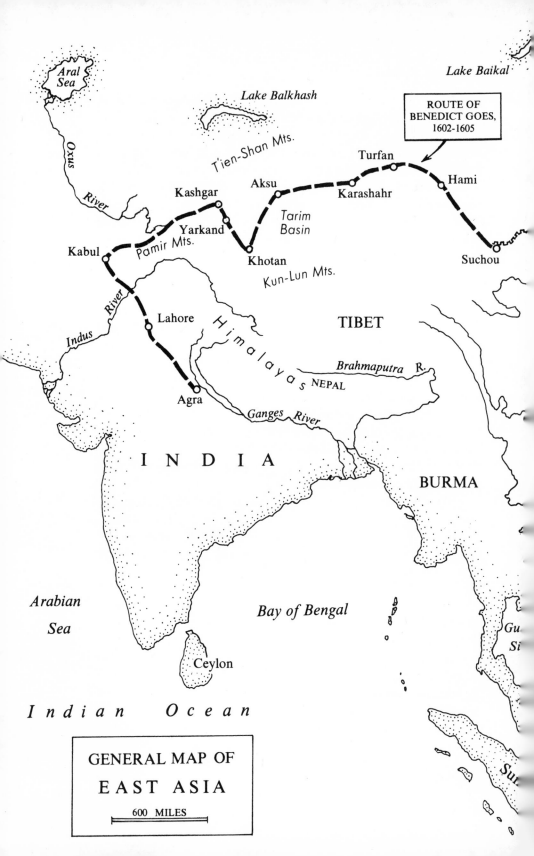

Aral
Sea

Lake Balkhash

Lake Baikal

ROUTE OF
BENEDICT GOES,
1602-1605

Oxus

Tien-Shan Mts.

Turfan

Hami

Kashgar

Aksu

Karashahr

River

Yarkand

*Tarim
Basin*

Kabul

Pamir Mts.

Khotan

Suchou

Kun-Lun Mts.

Indus

Lahore

TIBET

River

Himalayas

Brahmaputra R.

NEPAL

Agra

Ganges River

I N D I A

BURMA

*Arabian
Sea*

Bay of Bengal

Gu
Si

Ceylon

Indian   Ocean

Su

GENERAL MAP OF
EAST ASIA

600 MILES

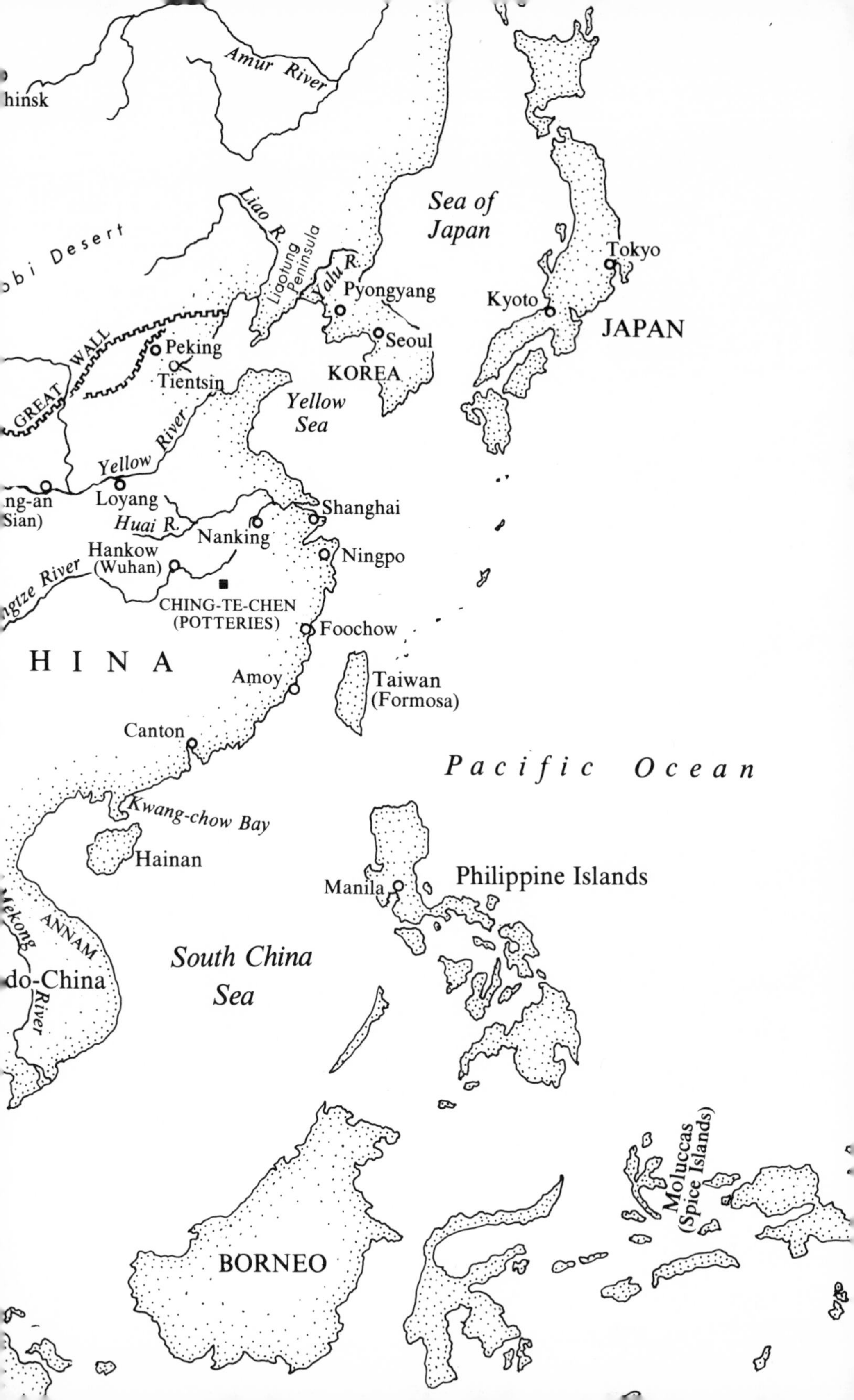
hinsk
Amur River
Liao R.
Gobi Desert
Liaotung Peninsula
Yalu R.
Sea of Japan
Tokyo
Pyongyang
Kyoto
JAPAN
Seoul
GREAT WALL
Peking
Tientsin
KOREA
Yellow Sea
Yellow River
ng-an
(Sian)
Loyang
Huai R.
Shanghai
Nanking
Hankow
(Wuhan)
Ningpo
ngtze River
CHING-TE-CHEN
(POTTERIES)
Foochow
H I N A
Amoy
Taiwan
(Formosa)
Canton
Pacific Ocean
Kwang-chow Bay
Hainan
Philippine Islands
Manila
ANNAM
Mekong River
South China Sea
do-China
Moluccas
(Spice Islands)
BORNEO

was his goal was the same China which Ricci had reached by sea. He was all the more impatient to be there. He and Issac traveled on with their caravan, through Turfan and Hami, then south across the desert. By the time they reached the outermost watchtower of the Great Wall, standing guard over the surrounding wilderness, it was the end of December, 1605, and Goes had been on his way for over three years.

Peking was still a thousand miles away. All travelers had to obtain permission from the Warden of the Gate to enter China and proceed to the capital, and now the Warden, possibly dissatisfied with the small amount of jade that Goes could offer him, refused to admit the two foreigners. After weeks of bargaining, they were finally allowed into China, but only as far as Suchou, a small city just inside the gate of the Great Wall.

There they stayed. Month after month went by. Goes sent letters to Father Ricci in Peking by every caravan that set out for the capital, but unfortunately he did not know Ricci's Chinese name, and it was a long time before one of these letters was actually delivered. Father Ricci then immediately sent a young Chinese lay brother, whose Christian name was John Ferdinand, to try to rescue the travelers. It was now midwinter, travel across north China was slow and difficult, and another four months had passed before John Ferdinand reached Suchou. He was only just in time. After over a year in Suchou, Goes, weakened by the hardships of the journey, by the fall from his horse and by undernourishment, was seriously ill, and he must have known in his heart that he would never see Peking. He died eleven days later.

Issac and John Ferdinand, although unable to understand a word of each other's language, held a Christian burial service for their master. There followed a tragi-comic epilogue when they had to prove in the Chinese law courts that they were Christians, or at least that they were not Moslems. If Issac had been a Moslem, the owners of the caravan with which he and Goes had traveled to Suchou, who had already seized what few possessions the two men had and destroyed all Goes' records and diaries, would have been able to claim him as their servant. The young Armenian was at his wits' end to convince the judges that he was neither Moslem nor Buddhist, belonging to a religion quite unknown to them, when John Ferdinand suddenly left the courtroom and came back carrying a dish of roast pork. He motioned to Issac, and the two of them sat down to eat it there and then.

The Chinese judges, much amused, promptly gave judgement in Issac's favor. Whatever the religion of these young men, they were certainly not Moslems; no Moslem would touch pork.

Issac and John Ferdinand, together, made their way to Peking, where they arrived on October 29, 1607, five years to the day after Goes had left Agra, and were warmly welcomed by the Jesuit fathers. Issac described in detail the journey from Lahore, in the land of the Great Mogul, to Suchou, within the walls of China; he outlined the route they had taken, the cities they had seen, the kingdoms along the way. He told of Goes' last days, explaining how and where he and John Ferdinand had buried him, hoping that some day there would be a monument over his grave. Although handicapped by the loss of the diaries, Father Ricci reported to his superiors everything that Issac told him. There was no doubt now that China was Cathay.

After some months' rest, the faithful Issac embarked on an almost equally adventurous journey by land to south China, and thence by sea to India, returning at last to his home in Lahore. No monument was ever built over the grave of Benedict Goes. Even the site is now unknown, but he is remembered by the words of a fellow Jesuit spoken on hearing of his death—"In seeking Cathay, he found Heaven."

5. Decline and

Fall of the Mings

Toward the end of the sixteenth century, the Ming Dynasty slowly disintegrated. There was an inevitability about its fall which seems to support the theory that there was a regular dynastic cycle in China; that each new dynasty enjoyed a hundred or even two hundred years of prosperity, and then decayed and died, like a living organism. It is a measure of the strength and the stabilty of the Ming Dynasty that it took so long to die.

Different factions fought to gain control over a series of weak and incompetent emperors. The central government lost touch with the provinces; reports of famine, flood and spreading discontent were conveniently suppressed. Corruption spread like a disease from the capital into provincial and district governments, and the honest, local gentry on whom so much of the local administration depended were powerless to stop it. There was no place for an honest man.

The most important single factor in the ruin of the Mings was the power of the eunuchs. Hung Wu, the founder of the dynasty, had foreseen this very danger. He had never allowed the court eunuchs to be educated, knowing that as long as they were illiterate they would only be employed as servants, and he had set up an inscribed stone tablet in the palace at Nanking warning his descendants against appointing eunuchs to any official position. The policy of Hung Wu was followed by his immediate successors, although there were one or two rare exceptions, such as the great Admiral Cheng Ho who commanded China's navy under Yung Lo. About 1430, however, the fifth emperor of the dynasty, a grandson of Yung Lo, started a school for the younger eunuchs in the palace, and before long they were being given a full education. It was a well-meaning gesture, with disastrous results.

The Chinese rulers regularly employed eunuchs to live and work in the harem, or Inner Courts, where other men were forbidden. These Inner Courts were a world of their own, inhabited by the emperor's wives, his numerous concubines and serving women, and his children; sons as well as daughters were brought up in the harem until they came of age. The system of concubinage was regarded as not only natural but virtuous and desirable; a man should have as many sons as possible, not only to help him in this life, but to carry on the ancestor worship which was essential to ensure the survival and comfort of his soul in the next world. Any man might have more than one wife, if he could afford it. The Emperor was expected to have several wives and senior concubines, with innumerable lesser concubines.

Since no man except the Emperor was allowed within the imperial harem, the eunuchs played an important part there, acting as guards, messengers, servants and companions to the women and their children. It was thought that the eunuchs, having no children of their own, would not be able to extend their influential positions in the harem from one generation to another, but, in fact, many eunuchs did establish hereditary power by adopting young boys of their own family to succeed them.

Hung Wu and Yung Lo, the founders of the Ming Dynasty, were men of action and independent mind, and were unlikely to be influenced by anyone else, certainly not by the palace eunuchs. But when the dynasty was well established, and the country at peace, the young princes—the future emperors— grew up almost entirely in the soft atmosphere of the Inner Courts. Isolated from the outside world, bored and lonely, they often became extremely attached to individual eunuchs. Once these were allowed an education, they also acted as tutors to the princes. If an emperor came to the throne young, it was only natural that he should choose his advisers from his former friends and tutors of the Inner Courts.

Although the eunuchs were often passionately loyal to their own master, they very rarely used their abilities or their influence for the good of the country. They enjoyed power without responsibility, often taking advantage of their position to build up enormous fortunes. The network of eunuchs which held power during the latter half of the Ming Dynasty, was entirely evil. Using their influence over the Inner Courts, over the Emperors' favorites and the Heirs Apparent to destroy all opposition in the palace, the eunuchs acted as a sort of secret police, virtually controlling the country. The Emperors themselves were often helpless in the face of their sinister organization.

If there had been any hope of reform, it was lost during the long reign of Wan Li (1573-1620). The name of Wan Li is familiar in the West because of the fine porcelain produced during his reign, and because his tomb, a huge marble palace buried seventy feet underground, was recently excavated by Chinese archeologists. Among its treasures were three marble thrones, gold, silver and porcelain ornaments, the Emperor's own swords and bow and arrow, as well as numerous large,

Example of Chinese calligraphy from a painting, Ming Dynasty.
THE METROPOLITAN MUSEUM OF ART (ROGERS FUND, 1946)

uncut pieces of fine jade. Wan Li's skeleton was found in a
crimson coffin; he had been wearing silk robes, a gold crown
and a wide belt of jade. (A government spokesman, stressing
the evils of China's imperial past, pointed out that the cost
of the tomb must have been equal to two years' national income
when it was built.)

Wan Li was not only extravagant; he was a weak character,
avaricious, sensual and quite uninterested in the welfare of his
people. His first Grand Secretary exercised a restraining influence, trying to introduce much-needed land and tax reforms,
but after his death the Emperor abandoned himself to a life
of luxury and pleasure that strained the country's resources
to the point of collapse. The eunuchs tightened their grip.
They now controlled the collection and spending of all public

funds, including those of the armed forces, which gave them enormous power.

Wan Li's heir died of arsenic poisoning, presumably given him by the eunuchs, within a few months of coming to the throne. His successor was a lad of fifteen, whose only real interest in life was carpentry; he enjoyed making fine lacquer furniture and once built a miniature palace in his gardens, furnished throughout with tiny lacquer tables, chairs and screens. Meanwhile, however, he left all government affairs in the hands of the eunuch Wei Chung-hsien, his childhood companion. Wei Chung-hsien ruled China, not hesitating to forge documents, destroy petitions to the Emperor and to assassinate those whom he could not bribe. He may have intended to found a new dynasty, for he insisted on being saluted wherever he went with cries of "Live Nine Thousand Years!" in imitation of the salute to the Emperor, "Live Ten Thousand Years!"

Wei Chung-hsien's control of the army so weakened it as a fighting force that law and order everywhere broke down. The White Lotus and other Secret Societies again gained power. At one time, the Emperor, on the advice of the Jesuits, appealed to the Portuguese at Macao for foreign gunners to help quell the disorders, and two hundred gunners actually reached Peking; Wei Chung-hsien, however, seeing his position threatened, insisted on the Portuguese being sent back to Macao without their guns ever having been used.

Loyal men, censors, scholars and civil servants, warned the Emperor again and again what was happening. One memorial to the throne listed twenty-four of Wei Chung-hsien's major crimes, including murder, torture and the forced abortion of the Empress when she might have given birth to a son. Their warnings were in vain. The Emperor remained blind to the end; when he was dying in 1627 and named his brother Ch'ung Cheng as his heir, he advised him to place implicit trust in Wei Chung-hsien.

Ch'ung Cheng, an honest man with no illusions about the difficulties facing him, knew better. He ordered Wei Chung-hsien and many of the other "rats and foxes," as the eunuchs were nicknamed, arrested and executed, trying to find loyal men to take their places. But it was too late. The Mings had thrown away the Mandate of Heaven. The brave censors, the men who had spoken out during the last two reigns, had been silenced. Corruption had become the only way of life at court and in government service.

Meanwhile, the tribes north of the Great Wall had united under the leadership of the Manchus. They had already invaded parts of north China, and Emperor Ch'ung Cheng had no choice but to keep his best trained and best equipped armies stationed along the Wall in defense of the northern frontier. This meant reducing his forces elsewhere, and, in fact, abandoning large areas of the south and west of the country to anarchy.

In these desperate times, many men took to the hills and became bandits. There were unpaid soldiers; there were farmers whose taxes were higher than the crops they could raise even in a good year; there were fugitives from the law, some innocent, some guilty. There were natural leaders among these men, and the starving and the discontented would follow them, until a so-called bandit might actually command several thousand men and control an entire province.

Such a man was Li Tzu-ch'eng, born about 1606. He was tall, and had the large, aquiline nose which in China is believed to be a sign of greatness; he was able, ambitious and supremely self-confident. The troops under his command, about one-third of whom were usually cavalry, were trained and equipped as a first-class fighting force. Those in the front line wore coats of "mail," folds and folds of overlapping padded silk which was proof against arrows, sword or spear. Even horses in the front line were protected with iron breastplates. The morale of the men was high; their discipline and organization was certainly superior to that of any imperial army south of the Great Wall.

Although Li Tzu-ch'eng could be unexpectedly generous, his campaigns were ruthless, and the terms he offered to the cities he besieged were like those of the Mongol hordes of four hundred years before. If a city surrendered immediately, its inhabitants would be spared, although it might be looted; if it resisted for one day, a third of the population would be massacred; after two days, two-thirds; after three days the entire population would be put to the sword. Once this was known, only the most strongly defended fortresses dared hold out against him.

Li Tzu-ch'eng was deeply superstitious. He was convinced that he had received the Mandate of Heaven, and he found many omens to confirm him in this belief. There was one old saying, widely quoted, that, "In the Year of the Monkey a one-eyed man will be King." In the cycle of twelve animals which give their names to successive years, 1644 would be the Year of the Monkey, and when during a battle which was fought in 1641 or 1642, an arrow pierced Li Tzu-ch'eng's left eye, he was delighted. Others also saw the significance of this; after the loss of his eye, he gained much wider support throughout the country.

District by district, city by city, Li's victorious armies, which are said to have numbered about three hundred thousand men, moved north. On New Year's day of the Year of the Monkey (February, 1644 in the Western calendar) he was in Sian, formerly Ch'ang-an, the great city which had been the strategic heart of ancient China, the capital of the Ch'in, the Han and the T'ang dynasties. There he announced the foundation of a new dynasty, the Ta Shun, or Great Obedient Dynasty, and crowned himself Son of Heaven.

Next, Li Tzu-ch'eng advanced upon Peking, where the Ming Emperor, Ch'ung Cheng still held the throne. In theory, the capital was strongly fortified and strongly defended. But of the thousands of soldiers whose names appeared on the lists, many were boys or old men, unarmed; others were on the payroll but had never existed, while others again were ready to desert to Li Tzu-ch'eng at the earliest opportunity. Li, whose spies went freely in and out of the city, was well aware of its weakness. On the walls of the Imperial City, so they told him, someone had scribbled the words—"If one star fall, let us follow another."

Ch'ung Cheng might still have saved the city if he had

ordered the troops stationed at the Great Wall to come to its defense, but to do so would have left the northern frontier wide open to the Manchus. As it was, he decided to man the walls of the capital with all the troops available there, and stand siege, which indeed the city was well equipped to do. Meanwhile, however, the commander-in-chief of the Peking garrison had already abandoned what he obviously considered a lost cause and had opened one of the gates in the outer city wall to Li Tzu-ch'eng's men. After that, it could only be a matter of hours before the Forbidden City itself fell to the rebels.

Ch'ung Cheng thereupon summoned his two eldest sons and ordered them to put on peasant clothes and escape from the city while there was still time, hoping that they would live to restore the dynasty. He sent word to the Empress and the senior concubines to kill themselves. Then he left the palace, followed by one faithful eunuch, and made his way in darkness through the deserted gates, gardens and courtyards of the Forbidden City until he reached its northern wall. From there he crossed into the grounds of Coal Hill, an artificial mound dotted with little pavilions, which overlooks the Forbidden City and was, in fact, built due north of the City to protect it from the baleful influences of the north wind.

The Emperor wrote a farewell message on the lapel of his inner coat: "Lacking in virtue, I have incurred the wrath of Heaven. The Ministers I trusted have deceived me. I am ashamed to face my ancestors. Therefore, removing my imperial cap, and with my hair dishevelled, I leave my body to the rebels. Let them not harm my people!" He and his companion then hanged themselves in a little pavilion on one side of Coal Hill. Thus died the last Chinese Emperor of China.

Li Tzu-ch'eng made a triumphal entry into Peking at noon on the same day, dressed in pale blue, with a golden cap and a gold sash, and riding his favorite piebald horse. As he approached the magnificent southern gate of the Forbidden City, with its massive tower (that same tower where Mao Tze-tung now stands on ceremonial occasions), he saw the characters

T'ien An Men, or Heavenly Peace Gate, carved above the entrance. He fitted an arrow to his bow.

"*T'ien* is the character for Heaven," he said to the men who crowded around him. "If I strike that sign full center it means that the Middle Kingdom is mine, in peace."

Although it was a comparatively easy shot, and Li was a fine marksman, he missed, and his arrow struck the wall just below the character. Superstitious as he was, he could not overlook such an evil omen; nor could other men. From that day, his good fortune deserted him.

6. The Manchu

Conquest

THE MANCHUS were a tribe of Juchen Tartars whose original home was north of Korea, northeast of China proper. Their sudden rise to power early in the seventeenth century was inspired by the leadership of their chief, Nurhachi, born in 1559. By patient negotiation as well as conquest, by marriage and by alliance, Nurhachi united the tribes of the Juchen under him. He also won the support of the Mongol tribes, now scattered and divided among themselves. Meanwhile, being favorably placed to trade with China, Korea and Central Asia, he established a sound economic basis for his rule; among other advantages, he secured a monopoly of ginseng, a root found in Korea and Manchuria which is highly valued among the Chinese for its medicinal properties. In 1616, he took the name of Manchu, the origin of which is unknown, for his territory and his people.

According to the annals of the Manchus, which of course show only one side of the picture, Nurhachi was willing to come to terms with the Ming rulers if they would recognize him as their equal, the ruler of an independent nation. When they would not—and as long as they maintained the fiction that the divinely appointed Son of Heaven ruled the world, they could not—Nurhachi declared war. In 1618, he addressed a list of grievances against the Chinese to the Ming Emperor, and then burned it, thus officially informing Heaven that a state of war existed.

By this time, the Manchus had a settled state with its capital near present-day Shen-yang, a government, a civil service, a powerful army and a written language. In 1599, Nurhachi had instructed two scholars to produce a script for the Manchu language, hitherto unwritten; it was based on the Mongol script, which in turn had been based upon the Syriac writing which Nestorian Christians had brought into Mongolia centuries before. Having a written language of their own made it easier to keep records and to run the government, while it also meant that the Confucian Classics and other Chinese works could be translated into Manchu. Nurhachi and his successors organized their society on Chinese lines, and employed many Chinese as civil servants; some of these were prisoners of war, but most had come over to the Manchus voluntarily, disillusioned by the corruption and folly of the Ming Dynasty.

The Manchu armies were never large, but they were highly trained. They were made up of companies of three hundred men who fought as a unit, the companies being grouped under one of four "Banners"—yellow, white, blue and red—to form banner corps of 7,500 men each. These original Banners were soon increased to eight; another eight were added to include the Mongol armies, and still another for Chinese who joined the Manchus against the Mings, making a total of twenty-four Banners. Although it was primarily a military organization, all Manchus were included under one or other of the Banners for purposes of taxation, conscription and so forth. The divisions were hereditary and were maintained throughout the Manchu Dynasty. At first an elite and a source of strength to the new state, toward the end of the dynasty, corrupt and idle Bannermen came to be one of the aspects of Manchu rule most hated by the Chinese.

Nurhachi died in 1626. He was succeeded by his son Abahai, under whose leadership the Manchus continued to flourish. In 1635, Abahai came into possession of the Great Seal of State of China, which had been lost in the Mongolian desert when the last Mongol Emperor fled from Peking in 1368, and had only recently been unearthed by a Mongol shepherd. The Manchus, although foreigners, therefore claimed that they had received the Mandate of Heaven, and Abahai gave his dynasty a Chinese name: Ch'ing, or Pure. His armies now ranged as far as the outskirts of Peking. The city itself, however, and, more important, the fortresses along the Great Wall were still strongly defended, and Abahai did not dare risk being cut off from his base.

To secure his flanks before the conquest of China, Abahai now demanded that the King of Korea transfer his allegiance from Ming to Manchu. When the King refused, Abahai marched into Korea at the head of a powerful army and reached the walls of the Korean capital in record time. The King very quickly changed his mind. He sent a herald out to welcome the invaders, expressing the hope that they were not tired after their long journey, and soon afterward he swore allegiance to the Manchu Dynasty.

Abahai died in 1643. His successor was his five-year-old son, later Emperor Shun Chih, but the leadership of the Manchus fell to another of Nurhachi's formidable sons, Dorgun, known in Chinese as Prince Jui. It was in the following year, as we have seen, that the rebel Li Tzu-ch'eng captured Peking, and the last Ming ruler hanged himself. Thus, while Li Tzu-ch'eng occupied Peking and much of north China, the Manchus in the north stood ready to invade the country whenever an opportunity presented itself. Between them, however, holding the

Great Wall, was a still powerful Chinese army, loyal to the fallen Ming Dynasty and commanded by an able, hot-tempered and extremely independent general, Wu San-kuei. Wu had been able to maintain the strength and discipline of his troops in spite of the general demoralization of the Chinese armies, because he was in such a strong position as defender of the Wall that he simply ignored the orders of the corrupt eunuch regime in Peking, and they could not touch him.

The Manchus would probably have conquered China in the long run against any defense. Li Tzu-ch'eng did not have the detailed organization of the Manchus, nor the whole-hearted support of the Chinese people. The Mings were scattered, their morale broken. Yet, as it turned out, it could be said in the words of Backhouse and Bland, that "The Manchus owed their dynasty, under Heaven, to the little singing-girl known to contemporary chroniclers as Lady Ch'en, the Round-faced Beauty."

At first, Wu San-kuei had been willing to come to terms with Li Tzu-ch'eng, if it were to his own advantage. In capturing Peking, however, Li had taken possession of Wu San-kuei's beautiful concubine, the Lady Ch'en, and held her in his own apartments, although whether as concubine or hostage is not clear. When he heard this, Wu San-kuei swore vengeance. He, whose entire life, and that of his father before him, had been spent in resisting the Manchus, now wrote to Dorgun, the Manchu Regent, and told him that he was determined at all costs to destroy the rebel armies of Li Tzu-ch'eng. He spoke in moving terms of his own weakness, and—weeping, as he said, tears of blood—begged the Manchus to come to his aid.

Dorgun must have read this letter with some surprise. The road to Peking not only now lay open to him—he was being urged to take it. In his reply, he spoke of his own grief at the death of the Ming Emperor, news of which had caused his hair to stand on end with horror, and promised help against the usurper. His horsemen, he said, were already moving south to join forces with Wu San-kuei. It was an eloquent letter. But it made clear that the Manchus would be the new rulers of

China; there was no question, as Wu may have hoped, of restoring the Ming Dynasty.

Li Tzu-ch'eng, meanwhile, unaware of Wu's agreement with the Manchus, and, therefore, believing his enemy to be caught between the Manchu armies and his own, took the initiative and advanced to within a few miles of the Great Wall. He was eager for battle and confident of victory in any engagement with Wu San-kuei. He had met and defeated other imperial Chinese armies before now; his forces were certainly larger than those of Wu, and his cavalry were the best-trained and best-equipped in China.

Wu San-kuei, with good reason, was equally confident as he marched out to meet the rebel forces in a valley south of the Wall. His men, who knew nothing of the promised Manchu support, were perhaps less sanguine. Scarcely had the two armies met when they were struck by a blinding dust storm, one of those sudden, fierce storms common to north China, so that the sky turned yellow and the soldiers were almost invisible to one another. Within a few hours, however, it was clear that Wu San-kuei's men, heavily outnumbered, were being driven back, with great loss of life on both sides.

Then at a given signal, the Manchu cavalry, twenty thousand strong, who had been hidden in the hills on either side of the valley, hurled themselves down the rocky slopes and fell upon Li Tzu-ch'eng's advancing army. Fine horsemen though they were, Li's cavalry were no match for the barbarians—whose native country, so it was said, was the back of a horse. To anyone as superstitious as Li moreover, taken by surprise in such a storm, it must have seemed that the legendary Dust Devils, who are said to inhabit the deserts of the north, had taken up arms against him. His men panicked, broke ranks and fled, scattering arms and equipment for miles behind them.

Li's ambitions and his dynasty were destroyed in that one battle. Returning to Peking, he stopped only long enough to execute a number of officials—including Wu San-kuei's father, whose head stuck on a spike over the city gate was the first sight that greeted Wu when he reached the capital a few days later—and then fled westward. His demoralized soldiers drifted away to fend for themselves. All but a few of his own men deserted him, and he himself is said to have been killed by some villagers during the retreat.

After the flight of Li Tzu-ch'eng, people in Peking believed that Wu San-kuei would be able to restore the Ming Heir Apparent to the throne. Instead, it was the Manchus who shortly appeared at the gates of the city, escorted by Wu San-kuei, and it was the Manchu Regent who stepped into the imperial chair provided for the new ruler. Soon afterward, the young Manchu boy-king, Nurhachi's grandson, was brought to Peking and formally installed as Shun Chih, first Emperor of the Ch'ing Dynasty.

The Manchus made every effort to appear as liberators rather than conquerors. They buried the unfortunate Ming Emperor Ch'ung Cheng with all the ceremonies which would have been performed by his legitimate heir. They introduced no major changes in the administration, or in the social and economic life of the country, and they maintained the all-important examination system by which government officials were chosen. In many ways, the culture, society and traditions of the Ming Dynasty flowed uninterrupted into the Ch'ing, remaining Chinese rather than Manchu.

Wu San-kuei had stipulated four conditions when he went over to the Manchus. The first was that Chinese women should not be taken into the imperial harem, a rule which was soon ignored. The second was that no Manchu should take first place in the great triennial examinations for the civil service. The third was that Chinese men, although they would wear Manchu dress and a queue, could be buried in the costume of the Mings. The

Hall of Annual Prayers, Temple of Heaven, Peking.
PHOTOGRAPH BY GILLIAN WILSON

fourth was that Chinese women need not wear Manchu dress, but that they should give up the custom of binding their feet. Extraordinary although it may seem now, this last idea met with so much opposition that the regulation concerning bound feet was withdrawn, and high-class Chinese women carried on with this excruciatingly painful process until the twentieth century.

The queue, which had been customary among the Manchus for some time, involved shaving the head except for a patch in

the center, where the hair was allowed to grow long and then braided. There was strong opposition at first among the Chinese to wearing the queue. Later, however, it became so natural to them that many Chinese insisted on retaining their queues (which foreigners sometimes called pigtails) even after the 1911 Revolution.

Manchu officials took over positions of authority in the government, but senior Chinese officials remained to work with them. Each Ministry had two presidents, one Manchu and one Chinese; and four vice-presidents, two Manchu and two Chinese. At first all the Ministries, the Secretariat and indeed the whole court had to be bilingual, but as time went on Manchu was used less and less in the administration. The Manchus learned Chinese, the Chinese did not bother to learn Manchu, and before long the latter was only used for Manchu affairs, or as a court language.

The Manchus drastically curtailed the power and the privileges of the eunuchs, employing them only as servants in the Inner Courts; it was to be well over a hundred years before they crept back into power again, although in the end they played almost as large a part in the downfall of the Manchus as they had with the Mings. As usual at the beginning of a new dynasty, taxes were reduced, and the newcomers concentrated on restoring and rebuilding roads, canals and other public works, and on famine relief. They did not strengthen the Great Wall, as other new regimes had done; with the Manchus ruling both China and Manchuria, the Wall was no longer needed for defense, although it was still considered the boundary of the Middle Kingdom and permission was still needed to cross it.

Thus the country recovered from the years of civil war, the anguish which had marked the disintegration of the Ming Dynasty, and entered into a new golden age. It did not happen overnight. However adaptable they might be, the Manchus were foreigners. The Ming Dynasty still had strong support in the south and Ming princes established rival governments, first in Nanking, then in Foochow, Canton and other cities. The most active leader in the long, bitter campaigns against these loyalists was none other than Wu San-kuei, now reunited with his beloved Lady Ch'en. Once the defender of the Ming Dynasty, he served the Manchus with equal devotion for thirty years. Yet in the end, he turned against them as he had against the Mings; in 1674, he proclaimed a new dynasty of his own in the southern provinces, a rebellion which was not put down until after his death four years later.

It was 1680 before the Manchus were in control of all mainland China. Even then resistance was not at an end. Loyalist Chinese forces held out for another three years on the island of Formosa, led by the descendants of one Koxinga, a colorful character without whom Formosa might never have belonged to China.

Koxinga was the ablest of four generations of the Cheng family, pirates who preyed on the south coast of China for many years. They were bandits, yet also patriots. China had no naval force to speak of at that time, and Koxinga's people, while raiding the Chinese coastline themselves, defended it from attack by the Japanese, Portuguese and other foreigners.

Koxinga's father was a strong supporter of the Ming Dynasty. The son spent much time at the refugee loyalist court at Nanking, where he became such a favorite that the Ming princes gave him their own surname, Chu (as in Chu Yüan-chang, founder of the dynasty), a most unusual honor. Thereafter, he was always called Lord of the Imperial Surname, or Kuo Hsing-yeh, which the Dutch pronounced Koxinga. He was bitterly opposed to the Manchus, attacking Manchu garrisons all along the south China coast, until at one time the government was forced to move the entire coastal population of some districts inland to safety. In 1661, he seized Formosa, driving out the Dutch who had occupied the island for the last thirty-five or forty years.

Koxinga died in 1662. His sons carried on the fight for another twenty years. It was not until 1683, by which time the Manchu Dynasty was well established and was building ships of its own, that the rebels agreed to surrender the island, on their own terms.

Thus Formosa the Beautiful (a Portuguese name; the Chinese and Japanese call the island Taiwan) became part of China. Had it not been for Koxinga, it would most likely have remained a Dutch colony. The Manchus seem to have recognized this, for once he was dead and no longer dangerous to them, they graciously agreed to Koxinga's being canonized as the guardian spirit of Formosa. He had not rebelled against them, the official memorial explained, he had simply persisted in his loyal, if misguided support of the former dynasty. Here in Taiwan, the memorial went on to say, he had built a new dominion out of what had been only a wilderness among the waters; he had handed this on to his descendants, and they in turn had loyally presented it to the Great Ch'ing Dynasty.

7. Ashikaga Japan

THE GEOGRAPHY, history and culture of Japan are very different from those of China. A string of islands, not a continent; a civilization that developed late, maturing quickly; a people eager to learn from foreigners and to adopt new ideas.

The prehistoric ancestors of the Japanese probably came in waves from the mainland of Asia, through Korea, mixing with other immigrants from the South Pacific. Their spoken language is unrelated to that of China. And even when Japan's much younger culture seemed to be copying Chinese ways, Chinese art, religion and form of government most slavishly, what emerged was recognizably Japanese. This has been true not only in art, religion and government but in food, clothing and shelter.

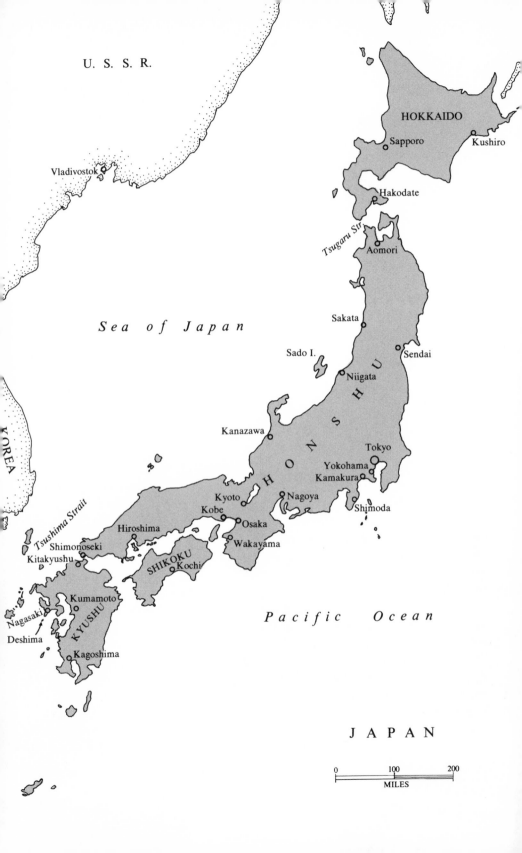

Although the staple diet of both is rice or other cereals, the simple Japanese cuisine is distinct from that of the Chinese, with its wide variety of sauces. The Japanese kimono, although adapted from Chinese dress of the eighth century, was quite unlike later Chinese styles. The Japanese wore split-toe socks with sandals or wooden clogs, but always with a thong dividing the big toe from the rest of the foot; the Chinese wore cloth shoes or boots, and the Koreans wore boots with turned-up toes. Japanese houses were built of wood, whereas Chinese and Korean homes were usually brick or mud.

The system of government which developed in Japan over the centuries was complicated. The Emperor, although believed to be descended from the Sun Goddess and therefore superior to all other men, seldom held real power. Even during the Heian period (794-1185), the government had usually been controlled by one or more powerful nobles, ruling in the name of the Emperor. Then, toward the end of the twelfth century, a long and bitter conflict between the two most powerful clans in the country ended with the triumph of Yoritomo of the Minamoto clan. Had this happened in China, Yoritomo would have founded a new dynasty, but in Japan such a thing was impossible. The Emperor could not forfeit his divine right to rule; there was no Mandate of Heaven which could pass to another man, and although there might be more than one branch of the imperial line, no outsider ever laid claim to the throne.

Instead, Yoritomo had set up a government in Kamakura, quite separate from the Emperor's court at Kyoto. He took the title of Sei-i-Tai-Shogun, or Barbarian-quelling General, an ancient name which signified the highest military command, and his government was, in effect, a military one; it was based on the support of the military class, who were called Samurai, throughout the country. The Emperor might go through the motions of government, but it was the Shogun who ruled. (This exalted but unresponsible position of the Emperor was to be of great importance in 1867, when Japan decided to modernize itself.)

The system worked remarkably well. The equivalent of the rise and fall of dynasties in China was the rise and fall of clans holding the Shogunate. Traditionally, these clans had to be related to the Minamoto; only those who claimed Minamoto descent could, or did, become Shoguns.

The first hereditary Shogunate, established by Yoritomo at Kamakura, held control of the country for well over a century. During that time Yoritomo's successors fought off the two Mongol invasions in 1274 and 1281. These invasions, however, and the threat of further invasions to come, severely damaged the country's economy. Victories against an invader brought no material gain. On the contrary. Taxes were increased; feudal lords who had gone into debt to raise armies had no hope of paying them off, and even the Buddhist priests, claiming that their prayers had raised the violent typhoons which twice defeated the Mongols, were bitter that they received no reward.

By the beginning of the fourteenth century, the government had lost control, and the ruling class, unable to cope with the situation, turned helplessly to pleasure and frivolity. The last of the Kamakura rulers, for instance, being amused by a dog fight, ordered such fights to be held every two or three days; the dogs taking part were treated like royalty, dressed in brocades, their kennels ornamented with gold and silver, and people had to kneel when they were carried in sedan chairs through the streets.

In this confused period a number of feudal lords, led by Ashikaga Takauji, attempted to restore power to the imperial line. Although they succeeded in overthrowing the government in Kamakura, these feudal leaders soon fell out among themselves, supporting different claimants to the imperial throne, and in the ensuing struggle for power Takauji was victorious. He then decided to become Shogun himself, and in 1336 he established the Ashikaga Shogunate. He was, however, by no means unopposed; he still had powerful enemies, and a complicated, many-sided struggle between rival factions resulted in almost sixty years of continuing intrigue and warfare before a compromise was reached in 1392.

Even after 1392, the Ashikaga never held the same position that the original Shoguns had enjoyed. Yoritomo and his successors had ruled through a feudal hierarchy, but the feudal lords had been their vassals; they were supported by their own liege men. Now, although they did not challenge the right of the Ashikaga to the title of Shogun, the lords and barons who acknowledged them as such owed no historical allegiance to the Ashikaga, and the latter never gained full control over them. Nor did they ever control the great Buddhist monasteries, which maintained armies of their own.

Many of the most powerful feudal lords thus remained virtually independent throughout the Ashikaga Shogunate. These were known as the Daimyo, or Great Names. They ruled their own territories almost without regard to the central government; their rivalry and the frequent quarrels among them sometimes led to minor civil wars, which the Shoguns were unable to prevent.

The first Ashikaga Shogun had intended to keep the government in Kamakura. Because of the continuing civil war, however, he established himself in the Muromachi district of Kyoto, and the government, in fact, remained there throughout the Ashikaga Shogunate. The period from 1392 to 1573 is often called the Muromachi.

The early years of the Muromachi were years of comparative peace and stable government. Economic growth was steady, as it had been through the thirteenth and fourteenth centuries. Even while the warlords and rival emperors fought, the country prospered. The true resources of the land, the rice fields, the timber, and above all the industriousness of its people, were little affected by the civil wars. Some peasants might be conscripted, but even among the soldiers, the loss of life was small, and the others went on about their business.

Not that the life of the Japanese peasant or farmer was ever an easy one. He had to battle against natural disasters so frequent that they were almost a part of daily life; typhoons, tidal waves, active volcanoes, monsoons whose fierce winds and rain might destroy his entire crop, and everlasting earthquakes.

(Disastrous earthquakes such as that of 1923 may be rare, but several thousand earthquake shocks are registered every year.) Japan, moreover, is a mountainous country, with less than twenty percent of its land suitable for cultivation. During the Middle Ages, and, indeed, until quite recently, the fields were small and the instruments in use were primitive—the hoe, the spade, the harrow and the sickle, with a plough scarcely different from that used in Egypt in the time of the Pharaohs. The most important element in all Japanese agriculture was the never-ending toil of the farmer himself.

Rice was always Japan's most widely cultivated crop, although wheat, millet and barley were also grown and were, in fact, the common food of the poor classes, rice being something of a luxury. Good quality rice needs flooded fields, and an immense amount of hand labor, first in hoeing the beds, then in building perforated mud dams and a complicated system of terraced irrigation ditches whereby water could be brought down gradually from one field to another. The growing season was long, with the rice often not being reaped until September or October, but during the Ashikaga period a strain of early-ripening rice was introduced from Indochina, and this meant that in some parts of the country a second crop, usually barley, could be planted after the rice was harvested.

The Japanese, like their Chinese neighbors, kept very few cattle; they considered milk to be a medicine rather than a food. They did, however, have an inexhaustible source of protein in the waters of their own archipelago, for the seas surrounding Japan abound in fish, shellfish and edible seaweed, all of which played a large part in the Japanese diet.

In early feudal times, rice had been the recognized form of currency throughout Japan. The feudal lords were almost self-sufficient, building their own houses, growing their own food, making their own pottery, farm utensils and weapons, and buying or bartering only a few items, such as salt or iron, which their estates could not produce. Now, however, in the fifteenth and sixteenth centuries, there was a great increase in the use of copper cash, and a corresponding increase in the demand for new and different things. Regular markets were held from three to six times a month. These would be set up along a well-traveled road or near the entrance to a monastery, and their stalls offered goods—practical items like pots and kettles, agricultural instruments, cloth, paper goods (paper had been invented in China about the second century A.D., and was now common in East Asia), bows and arrows, rice, fish, vegetables and dried fruits, sesame oil for lamps or for cooking, and more frivolous items such as rouge and eyebrow pencils—all in exchange for cash.

The copper coins were imported from China. They were declared legal tender as early as 1226. During the Mongol occupation of China, this trade was interrupted, and there was a shortage of coins, but it was resumed again at the end of the fourteenth century. By that time the Japanese had started producing inferior counterfeit coins of their own, and the currency was officially classified as "good," "medium" or "bad."

The founding of the Ming Dynasty in China in 1368 coincided with the accession of Yoshimitsu, the third Ashigaka Shogun, and one of the ablest. Both Yoshimitsu and the Ming Emperor, Hung Wu were anxious to reestablish good relations, although for somewhat different reasons. Yoshimitsu needed the money that trade with China would bring, while Hung Wu hoped that Japan would become a tributary of China's, and that this might make it easier to control the Japanese pirates who infested China's coastline.

Around the turn of the century, Hung Wu and Yoshimitsu exchanged flowery letters and an increasing number of ambassadors, Buddhist monks and trade missions. Japan sent swords and armor, horses and sulphur to the continent, and received, in return, a few luxuries such as sandalwood, incense and jade, as well as large quantities of the copper coins on which their growing economy depended.

Yoshimitsu is criticized by Japanese historians because he did not correct the Chinese Emperor when the latter addressed him as King of Japan, and because he sent tribute to China. But this was largely a matter of words. As far as the Chinese knew,

Yoshimitsu was the ruler of the country, and it was natural to call him King; while anything a Chinese Emperor received was called tribute, even if he sent back goods of greater value in exchange.

Yoshimitsu and his successors were great collectors of Chinese art; it is because of their extravagant love of beauty and of things Chinese that Japan has such a wealth of ancient Chinese paintings and porcelains. He built several magnificent palaces to house his Chinese collections, but he is best remembered for a simple, three-storied building overlooking a small lake near Kyoto, and known as the Kinkaku, or Golden Pavilion. (This was unfortunately destroyed by fire in 1952; rebuilt, it seems to have lost much of its original character.) The Kinkaku was not only beautifully proportioned but it blended perfectly with its natural setting—the lake, the trees and the hillsides amongst which it stood. It was of a sophisticated, deliberate simplicity peculiar to Japan, and especially to the Muromachi. This simplicity was achieved by devoting endless effort, thought and patience to producing something so "natural" that it seemed to have grown of itself. It is sometimes called the Cultivation of the Little, a style which sees a single flower as more beautiful than a garden; bare, polished wood as more valuable than fine lacquer.

Yoshimasa, the eighth Shogun, who succeeded in 1443, also had a deep understanding of art and a lasting influence. The style and furnishings of his court were enthusiastically copied by the feudal lords, even those ruling in the remote western provinces of Japan. Against the background of independent feudal estates, with little or no central government, the country was, nevertheless, culturally homogeneous; a truly national art developed, and Muromachi is remembered as one of the great ages of Japanese culture.

Yoshimasa built a Silver Pavilion to rival Yoshimitsu's Golden Pavilion, and it was here that the tea ceremony was perfected. The object of this ceremony is the contemplation of beauty. A few friends will meet in a small room, unfurnished except for a single painting, or perhaps a bowl of flowers, where the tea will be made by a tea master. Every instrument the master uses, the whisk, the bowl, the cups, must be simple but perfect of its kind, so that those sharing in the ritual are lost in calm enjoyment of its perfection. They may then discuss the merits of a painting, the color of a bowl or the beauty of an unpolished wooden ladle. Their minds are refreshed, their senses heightened. It is true that men often spent a fortune on the "simple" objects they so admired, but the idea behind the ceremony remained the appreciation of beauty in form and color, and a brief withdrawal from worldly cares.

The No Dance, combining poetry, music and dancing in an art quite unlike anything else, was also developed in the time of Yoshimitsu and Yoshimasa. The bare floor-boards of the No theater, and the lack of all scenery except three symbolic pine trees, reflect the underlying austerity of Japanese taste. The action is slow and formal, accompanied by a chorus which is seated at one side, and sometimes by drum and flute. The costumes, however, are incredibly rich—heavy silks and brocades, in bright color and elaborate design, one robe often half-concealing another; these contrast with the simplicity of the setting, and emphasize the stiff movements of the actors.

The master painters of the Muromachi drew their inspiration from China, not from contemporary work there but from earlier painters, especially those of the Sung Dynasty. Very soon, however, they developed a character of their own, which is well expressed in the landscapes of the Kano school of painting. Individual Japanese painters of the fifteenth century, among them Josetsu, Shubun and especially Sesshu (1420-1506) were certainly the equals of any contemporary Chinese artist. Their genius lay in capturing the whole, wild beauty of nature in a few brush-strokes, the winding river in a single eddy of water, the depth of the forest in a tree. Their apparently simple ink-paintings are masterpieces.

The austerity of the tea ceremony, the No Dance and of Japanese architecture and painting at this time was partly due to the influence of Zen Buddhism. Zen, a sect which had begun in China and took root in Japan during the twelfth and thir-

teenth centuries, teaches that salvation and enlightenment are to be found only within oneself, by meditation, strict physical and mental discipline, and absolute self-control. It is closer in feeling to the native Shinto religion of Japan, with its simple faith and its near-worship of nature, than other Buddhist sects, and it was well suited to the Japanese temperament. Unworldly although its doctrines may seem, its emphasis on discipline and self-reliance appealed equally to the artists and the warrior class. Many leaders, Shogun Yoshimitsu among them, were inspired by this faith.

The mixture of militarism with genuine piety is reflected in a strange episode concerning Yoshimitsu and the Japanese pirates. These pirates operated against Korea as well as China, and at the beginning of the fifteenth century, the King of Chosen (Korea) begged Yoshimitsu to return certain hostages who had been carried off by the freebooters. Yoshimitsu replied that he would willingly return the hostages, but he wanted payment in advance: a complete copy of the Tripitaka, or sacred books of Buddhism, which the Koreans had recently printed from woodblocks. It was no small thing to ask. There were 162,516 pages in these books, and printing them was a great work.

Yoshimitsu's successors made the same request. They received no answer until 1423, fifteen years after Yoshimitsu's death, when a set of the books unexpectedly arrived in Japan, with a renewed request for the return of the hostages. The missing Koreans, or at least those who were still alive and could be found, were then repatriated.

Yoshimitsu did have some success against the Japanese pirates. He destroyed several of their bases, and on one occasion he boiled a dozen or so pirates alive in huge copper kettles as

"Winter Landscape," by Sesshu (1420–1506).

an example to the others. But it was impossible to eliminate them altogether. There were many harbors along the west coast of Japan where the pirate ships could hide and from which they could make surprise landings on the Chinese or Korean coast. Such ships carried up to two or three hundred men, whose great swords were the terror of the China seas. They looted anything and everything they found—grain, copper coins, silk, furniture and weapons, and they also took prisoners to be sold as slaves in Japan. (Slavery, although illegal, persisted in Japan throughout the Ashikaga period.)

The Japanese, moreover, may not have wanted to get rid of the pirates altogether. They were never sure of China's peaceful intentions—they had, after all, fought off two invasions from the mainland during the thirteenth century—and they may have been glad to have ships manned by adventurous, tough and armed men operating from their islands. A somewhat similar situation existed in sixteenth-century England, when Drake and other gallant captains might be looked upon as daring navigators, or as pirates, depending on the point of view and on their activities at the time.

The treasure brought back by these pirates was welcome in Japan. The Ashikaga Shoguns, for all their emphasis on simplicity in art, were incredibly extravagant, and the pomp and luxury of their courts laid an ever-increasing burden on the country. Even new and onerous forms of taxation failed to meet their demands.

The burden of these taxes inevitably fell on the lower classes. The Japanese class system was rigid. The Samurai, or warrior class, stood high above the others, followed by farmers, artisans and merchants, this being the order in which they were considered useful to society. Quite apart from these classes were the untouchables, outcasts whose occupations were considered degrading or religiously impure; these included the executioners, butchers and leather-workers, since their work violated the Buddhist laws against taking life, and men who catered to the amusement of others, from brothel-keepers to snake-charmers, acrobats and beggars.

The peasant or farm-worker was thus high in the social scale, even as in China. In general, however, as we have seen, their life was a constant struggle against the elements and the demands of their masters, so that the artisans and the despised merchant class usually lived very much better than they did. When excessive taxation coincided with natural disasters and civil war, even the long-suffering Japanese peasant was driven to revolt. A series of peasant uprisings during the fifteenth century were ruthlessly suppressed, as were others in later years, but they did draw attention to the grievances of the lower classes, and in some cases the Shoguns did reduce taxation or even punish an oppressive feudal lord. (This did not always benefit the rebels themselves. One brave farmer who presented a memorial to the Shogun on behalf of several hundred fellow workers during the seventeenth century was forced to see his children beheaded, before he and his wife were crucified; it was only after this that the Daimyo who had been responsible for their sufferings was found guilty and punished.)

Shogun Yoshimasa, that discerning patron of the arts, was not a strong ruler. Even a stronger man might not have been able to prevent the disastrous Onin War which broke out in 1467 between two rival lords, a senseless quarrel which dragged on for eleven years, and which was fought in the streets and palaces of Kyoto itself. That beautiful city was almost completely destroyed, and contemporary writers speak of empty wastes where palaces and monasteries had stood, now become the haunt of wolves and foxes.

The Onin War was followed by another century of strife, the Age of the Country at War. It is not easy to follow the threads of this conflict, nor understand the bitter struggles among the Daimyo, who acknowledged no authority other than their own. No leader was able to bring them together; the idea of a single nation, under one rule, seemed to have been lost.

Yet the pattern of society was changing in such a way as to make the country more united. Many of the feudal lords now realized that they could strengthen their own position by recruiting not only unemployed fighting men but also poor or landless peasants for military service. In return for employment, security and protection, they won the allegiance and loyalty of the peasants. They could only do so, however, by treating these recruits well; otherwise they would transfer their allegiance to some neighboring lord, where they would also be welcome, and for the same reasons. This led to a healthy rivalry in providing good terms of service, living conditions and just treatment for the soldiers. It also meant that from about the end of the sixteenth century onward it was easier for a poor man, of peasant origin but with outstanding qualities, to rise to a position of some influence in the country. For the time being, the patriotism of these men was local, to their own liege lord, but in the long run, they were to play a major part in uniting the country and inspiring a truly national patriotism.

Meanwhile, the distinction between the classes other than Samurai was fading. Merchants and small landowners played an increasingly important part in the life of the country, both economic and social. New towns and cities were developing a life of their own. Roads and communications had improved enormously, and as more people traveled, they carried new ideas with them. The provinces were becoming increasingly self-sufficient and independent of Kyoto, a tendency hastened by the ruin of the capital during the Onin War. Under the surface, obscured by feudal rivalries and squabbles, the divided country was growing together.

8. Reunification

of Japan

THE URGE for national unity found expression in three great leaders: Nobunaga, Hideyoshi and Ieyasu. Although they succeeded one another as dictators, the three were nearly contemporaries in age; Nobunaga was born in 1534, Hideyoshi in 1536 and Ieyasu in 1542. They were men of very different character, as illustrated by three famous couplets describing their reactions to a songbird which remained obstinately silent. "If that bird does not sing, I will wring its neck," said Nobunaga; "If that bird does not sing, I will make it sing," said Hideyoshi; "If the bird does not sing, I will wait until it does," Ieyasu promised.

Nobunaga was ruthless and eccentric, with a violent temper.

As a youth he was so wild that his tutor committed suicide in the hope of bringing his undoubtedly able pupil to his senses, and it is said that this typically Japanese gesture changed Nobunaga's life. Hideyoshi was a man of humble birth, small in stature and ugly, with a monkey-like face—a most unlikely character to have become, as he did, not only the first commoner in Japanese history to rise to the highest position in the state, but the first man in several centuries to rule the whole of Japan. Ieyasu was, perhaps, more far-seeing than the others, working toward a form of government which would keep Japan united long after his own lifetime.

Nobunaga inherited a small estate in central Japan. His qualities soon attracted the attention of Hideyoshi, who knew that the quickest way of furthering his own ambitions would be to serve under a strong leader, and who, therefore, joined Nobunaga as a humble groom or foot-soldier in about 1558. Two years later Nobunaga won a crucial battle against the far superior forces of a rival lord, and Hideyoshi apparently played a major part in the victory; thereafter he became Nobunaga's leading commander in the field. Meanwhile, the battle of 1560 had another important result. Tokugawa Ieyasu, a minor chieftain in the opposing army, and only eighteen at the time, also decided to join forces with Nobunaga.

Nobunaga now rapidly expanded his estates, sometimes by force, more often by diplomacy and intermarriage among the rival Daimyo, until he was among the most powerful of these. He was one of the first to take advantage of the fire-power of the new muskets, copied from those of the Portuguese, which Japanese gunsmiths were now producing. Before long his reputation was such that the Emperor secretly urged him to occupy the capital, Kyoto, which had been for many years in a state of anarchy, and to restore order there. In 1568, after some hesitation, he did so. Emperor and Shogun retained their titles, but Nobunaga, as Vice-Shogun, became the real master of Kyoto and of central Japan.

Outside this area were the great estates of other independent feudal lords, owing allegiance to no one. Ieyasu now campaigned against these barons in the east, as did Hideyoshi in the west, and one by one, by strategy and force, they overcame leaders who were often more powerful than themselves. Nobunaga was generous to those who accepted his terms. He was, however, completely ruthless towards the Buddhist monasteries, many of which were strongly fortified, with their own independent armies, and were in the habit of taking sides with one feudal lord against another. Monasteries which refused to surrender were besieged; many were destroyed by fire and their inhabitants massacred. The military power of the priesthood, and with it their political influence, was destroyed once and for all.

Nobunaga was murdered in 1582 by one of his own generals, who is said to have been insulted because Nobunaga in a light-hearted moment struck him on the head with a fan, although the quarrel doubtless went deeper than that. On hearing of Nobunaga's death, Hideyoshi hurried back to the capital, defeated the assassin's forces in a single battle, and took command.

The loss of Nobunaga almost led to civil war between Hideyoshi and Ieyasu. Both men, however, were so determined to bring the other warring Daimyo under control and to unite Japan that they soon came to terms with one another. Hideyoshi, although he was never called Shogun, not being of Minamoto blood, became Regent and dictator, and Ieyasu served him loyally until his death. Together they continued their conquest of the country, until by 1590, Hideyoshi was the unquestioned master of all Japan, with his headquarters at Edo, the modern Tokyo. Kyoto, now restored, remained the imperial capital.

The courts of Nobunaga and Hideyoshi were very different from those of their predecessors. Gone were the bare wooden walls, the simple pavilions, the austere beauty so admired by the leaders of the Ashikaga or Muromachi period. The new rulers were unimpressed by the refinement of Kyoto; they wanted color, size, magnificence. Their castles were monumental structures, rising behind thick, stone walls and wide moats. (This was also due to the introduction of firearms, and the consequent need for stronger defenses.) Their interiors were bright with gold and gold leaf, red lacquer and elaborately painted wood-carvings. Artists reflected the taste of the day in their brilliant screens and wall paintings, exuberant landscapes and an increasing use of human figures.

Hideyoshi was outstanding as both statesman and general, with a great gift for inspiring loyalty in those who served him. He was a keen judge of men and often succeeded in winning his enemies over by argument, or by strategy, using force only as a last resort. During his campaigns he kept himself informed on conditions throughout the country, on food supplies, on the strength of possible opposition, and—perhaps most important— on the character of other leaders and their troops, so that he could play on the jealousy of one noble for another, or exploit dissatisfaction among the soldiers. His intelligence service proved equally useful when the country was at peace.

Once supreme in Japan, however, Hideyoshi's ambition led him into an adventure for which he could not be so well prepared. He decided to conquer China. The weakness of the Ming Dynasty at the time, and the ease with which pirate ships landed on the China coast, may well have led him to under-estimate China's strength. Moreover, he probably did not appre-ciate all the difficulties involved in the invasion of a country by sea.

At the same time, he may have wanted some foreign ad-venture to distract his own people. The measures by which Nobunaga and Hideyoshi had established control over the country had caused grave discontent. Farmers and small land-owners were left with less land and higher taxes. A national land

survey and a census restricted their freedom of movement, making it easier to conscript their labor. The Sword Hunt in 1588 forced people to give up the arms they were in the habit of carrying; it was small comfort to them to be told that the metal would be used for a new Great Image of Buddha, so that those who lost their weapons might save their souls. The nobles, too, had their grievances; their castles and fortresses were demolished, and their estates divided, so that no Daimyo should be strong enough to challenge the central government.

Hideyoshi's strategy was to invade China by way of Korea. When the Koreans refused to allow his troops free passage, he ordered a preliminary invasion of the Korean Peninsula. The expedition consisted of two hundred thousand men, with another hundred thousand in reserve, fully equipped with arms, provisions, transport ships, and an escort of warships, and financed by a special issue of gold and silver coins. It was led by his most experienced commanders; Hideyoshi himself did not take part in the invasions.

The first Japanese troops landing on the Korean coast in 1592 met with little resistance, and advanced so rapidly up the Korean peninsula that they were in danger of being cut off from their supplies. Like the Mongols, however, they were defeated by the sea. It was the Korean navy, under Admiral Yi Sun-sin, which decided the fate of the Japanese invasion.

Yi Sun-sin was not only a great seaman; he had designed and built a new type of vessel, said to be the first iron-clad ship in naval history. (Iron-clad warships were not built in the West until the nineteenth century, and their first use in action there was the battle between the Merrimac and the Monitor during the American Civil War.) We should remember that the Japanese ships of the time were open and unarmed, making up for this by their aggressiveness in attack and their crews armed with muskets, swords, bows-and-arrows and fire-arrows which could set an enemy ship alight. The Chinese, in their desperate resistance against Japanese pirates, had been experimenting with a curved wooden roof above the main deck of their ships, like the shell of a turtle. Yi Sun-sin carried this idea further by covering the wooden shell with sheet iron, leaving only narrow portholes through which fire-arrows could be shot, and adding pointed iron spikes to prevent boarding. Prow and stern alike were strengthened with metal to serve as battering rams. Once, at least, Yi Sun-sin feigned retreat until the Japanese were on his stern. Then he ordered the rowers to reverse oars, the stern became the bow, and he rammed a number of enemy boats before they could turn.

Although it is unlikely that the Japanese could have conquered China in the sixteenth century, it was exceptionally bad luck for them to encounter such a man and such a ship in their invasion of Korea. The Turtle Ships, as they were called, did incredible damage to the Japanese fleet. There seems to have been only one iron-clad Turtle, but most of the other Korean ships had at least a wooden roof. The Koreans also had, of course, the advantage of being familiar with the high tides and dangerous shoals of their own coastline. In a series of encounters over several weeks, Yi Sun-sin virtually destroyed not only the convoys bringing up supplies and reinforcements but the Japanese navy. On land, meanwhile, the Chinese had sent troops across the Yalu River, and the Japanese, suffering from cold, epidemics and increasing attacks from Korean guerrillas, were slowly driven back. Within a year of their landing, the invaders withdrew.

Hideyoshi, while carrying on half-hearted peace negotiations with China, hastened to build a new fleet. In 1596, angered by the condescending attitude of the Chinese Emperor, he ordered a second invasion of Korea. This time the situation was reversed. The Japanese armies on land met with strong Chinese and Korean resistance, while their navy was almost unopposed. The reason was simple: Yi Sun-sin's successes had aroused such jealousy at court that the King had been persuaded to replace him with another man, a man so incompetent that he allowed the Korean navy, literally, to fall apart.

The struggle might have dragged on longer had it not been for Hideyoshi's death in 1598, when the invasion was abandoned. By that time, Yi Sun-sin had been restored to command,

and, with the few ships available, he ambushed the retreating troopships and their escort, scattered the convoy and sank several warships. It was his last exploit. The great admiral was killed during the battle, but not before he had experienced the satisfaction of seeing the last Japanese ship fleeing from Korean waters.

Hideyoshi, aged 62, died a natural death, his later years marred by frequent wild rages which seemed alien to his character. He may have suffered from mental disorder—possessed by a fox spirit, the Japanese said—which would also explain his ill-fated invasions of Korea. His five-year old son was named heir, and once again civil war threatened, but in 1600 Ieyasu won a major battle against his opponents and became master of Japan. Hideyoshi's son and his supporters held out for another sixteen years in the strongly fortified castle at Osaka, until they, too, were finally overcome in a bloody siege in 1616.

Ieyasu was soon granted that title of Shogun which Hideyoshi had never received. So began the Tokugawa Shogunate, with its headquarters at Edo—Tokugawa being the family name of Ieyasu. A major distribution of land was carried out, giving large estates between Kyoto and Edo to three of Ieyasu's sons and rewarding the nobles who had remained loyal to him with hereditary fiefs strategically located in central Japan. The new Shogun thus made sure that the heart of the country was under his control.

It was now that the doctrines of Confucius, already well known in Japan, became important in the government. Ieyasu and his advisers were determined to build a state that not even the most powerful combination of Daimyo could challenge. They were determined to divert the energies of the warrior class, the natural leaders of the country, from fighting to peace-

Castle, Osaka. JAPAN INFORMATION CENTRE, LONDON

ful pursuits. The Shogun, as dictator, would then be supported by a privileged military class who provided leadership for the people but who did not question the supremacy of their ruler. The Rules for the Military Houses which Ieyasu announced in 1615 were designed to this end, stressing that military men must combine intellectual studies on the one hand with warlike pursuits on the other; they must lead austere and virtuous lives, enforce the law, keep the peace and, incidentally, refrain from building new castles or strongholds without the express permission of the Shogun.

This social structure needed a moral basis. Buddhism, although it remained the faith of the people, had lost much of its spiritual and intellectual vigor, and in China, Korea and Japan alike, was entering on a period of decline from which it has never fully recovered. Shinto was a gentle, flexible religion of nature, not a code of conduct. Confucianism on the other hand, with its emphasis on loyalty and its fixed relationships— the master a master, the servant a servant—provided exactly the right framework for such a state and government. Confucian thought was to dominate the intellectual life of the Japanese ruling classes throughout the Tokugawa era.

There was, however, more than one way of interpreting Confucius. Here, again, Japan differed from China. Although there was undoubtedly some opposition in China to the orthodox Confucianism of the twelfth-century philosopher Chu Hsi, opposition led by Wang Yang-ming (1472-1529) among others, such opposition was not a major influence in Chinese thought. In Japan, the school of O Yomei, as Wang Yang-ming was called there, was an important movement, attracting Japanese scholars, reformers and political leaders, men of character and moral courage.

Chu Hsi had stressed study and knowledge as the first essential to every thought and every action; over the years the teachings of his school had become extremely rigid and conservative. O Yomei, on the contrary, taught that a man's own conscience, meditation and personal discipline were more important than anything to be learned in books, useful although such learning might be. It encouraged independent thought and idealism. This was closer in feeling to Zen Buddhism, and even to Shinto, than the classical interpretations of Confucianism and had a much greater appeal to the Japanese.

Later, such independence of thought led people to question the whole moral basis for the rule of the Shoguns, but for the time being Confucianism served them well.

9. Early Relations

with the West

I N 1542 OR 1543, the Great Wind which so often played a
part in Japanese history brought the first Europeans to
Japan. A Chinese ship on which three Portuguese sailors were
traveling to Macao was blown off course by a typhoon and
landed on a small island near Kyushu, where the foreigners
were hospitably received and entertained before being allowed
to continue their journey. The Japanese were especially intrigued by the smooth-bore muskets these Portuguese carried,
firearms being unknown in Japan, and such muskets were soon
being enthusiastically copied in Japanese smithies.

Portuguese merchants and Jesuit priests alike were quick to
explore this new world. Traders from Macao were soon sailing
into Japanese ports, competing for Japanese customers. And

when Francis Xavier, the Apostle of the Indies, landed in Japan in 1549, he was so impressed by the character of the Japanese that he believed the entire country might well become Christian. As we have seen, he came to the conclusion that he must first convert China, whereupon Japan would follow suit, and it was while trying to reach China that he died, but many other Jesuits carried on his work in Japan.

The Portuguese had the field to themselves for half a century, when they were followed by the Spanish; the Dutch and the British came later. And there was an important difference between these two groups. The Portuguese and the Spanish, Roman Catholics, were as eager to convert the Japanese to their faith as they were to trade with them; the Protestant English and Dutch were interested only in commerce, not converts.

The fact that trade and missionary activity were so inseparable among the early Europeans in Japan goes far to explain the changing attitude of the Japanese leaders toward them. The Japanese were friendly toward foreigners; they had absorbed Chinese culture, and they were willing to learn from the West. Christianity also appealed to them, although many people at first believed it to be a new form of Buddhism, which could coexist with other faiths. From the very beginning Christian converts were numerous, some genuine, some hoping for a greater share of foreign trade if they adopted the religion of the foreigners.

The persecution of the Christians came later, when Japanese rulers realized that the Christianity preached by the Catholic missionaries of that zealous age was not only an extremely narrow, intolerant religion, but that it might be dangerous to them. Its insistence on the supremacy of a foreign god undermined the authority of the government. Hideyoshi is said to have asked the pilot of one Spanish ship, who had been boasting of the great Spanish dominions, how his king had succeeded in conquering so many countries. The pilot explained that these had first been converted to Christianity, and that the Spanish armies, therefore, met with no opposition when they landed. This, it may be imagined, did little to reassure Hideyoshi, who had already noticed that Catholic priests demanded absolute loyalty and absolute obedience from their converts, expecting them to choose their religion rather than their Shogun if they had to make a choice.

Nobunaga, with his hatred of Buddhism and Buddhist priests, had favored the Christians and received them at court. He enjoyed the company of the foreigners and the stories they told of their own distant and very different worlds. The Japanese were intrigued by anything new, and although they never adopted western culture as they had the Chinese, they welcomed the increasing number of Portuguese ships trading along their coasts. They were interested not only in the firearms, the cannon and the muskets, that these carried but also in the watches and the clocks of the Europeans, in their maps of the world, their musical instruments and indeed anything that was new and curious in their eyes.

Not all these ships' cargoes were of western origin, for they also carried spices from Southeast Asia, and products of the New World. Potatoes and tobacco were among the crops introduced to Japan by foreign traders at this time. Smoking tobacco soon became a popular craze; it was prohibited in 1609 as a fire hazard, but the prohibition had little effect, and tobacco continued to be freely smuggled into the country.

Hideyoshi seemed equally well disposed to the foreigners when he first came to power. In 1587, however, although not banning Portuguese trade, he ordered all Christian missionaries to leave Japan. Like the prohibition on tobacco, his edict was not very strictly enforced in the beginning; the missionaries made themselves inconspicuous, many of the feudal lords gave them shelter and the authorities simply ignored them. Ten years later, by which time Japanese Christians numbered some 300,000, persecution began in earnest, although even then it was mild by comparison with religious intolerance in Europe at that same time. Three Portuguese Jesuits, six Spanish Franciscans and seventeen Japanese converts were put to death in 1597.

Shogun Ieyasu, who was anxious to build up a strong Japanese navy and merchant fleet, tolerated the Catholic missionaries because he wanted to attract the foreign trade and foreign ships which came with them. Yet he, too, saw the danger of their political activities, and issued a number of edicts against Christianity. He was also disillusioned by the arrogance and intolerance of many of the missionaries, and by the constant feuds between members of the Jesuit and Franciscan Orders of the Catholic Church.

In 1600, one Will Adams, an Englishman from Kent, who was the chief pilot of a fleet of Dutch ships, was driven off course and landed on the Japanese coast. As far as is known, he was the first Englishman to set foot in Japan. The Portuguese and Spaniards in Edo urged Ieyasu to have this stranger put to death, on the grounds that all Englishmen were pirates. Ieyasu, however, had Adams brought before him to see what kind of a man he might be, and he was so impressed by the Englishman's knowledge of ships and the sea, of gunnery, mathematics and geography, that he made him his adviser on naval affairs. A truly remarkable friendship developed between this Kentish seaman and the Shogun. Ieyasu came to rely on his advice not only in maritime matters but in all foreign affairs, and although the homesick sailor sometimes begged leave to return to England, the Shogun would not hear of it; he insisted that Adams remain permanently at the Japanese court. He did, however, present the Englishman with a house and an estate of his own, and a Japanese wife, as well as the privilege, generally reserved to Samurai, of wearing two swords.

After Ieyasu's death in 1616, the persecution of Christians was ruthless. The Shoguns, seeing that Christianity could be a tool in the hands of rebellious nobles, were determined to wipe out every trace of the religion in Japan. Torture and death were commonplace, and the list of martyrs grew long. The end came when what began as a local uprising in the western provinces became a last-ditch stand of Christians against anti-Christians. The rebels, fighting desperately, held out for three months at Shimabara, near Nagasaki. Bombarded from the sea, as well as from land, this stronghold finally fell in 1638, and over thirty thousand Christians, men, women and children, were massacred.

The courage with which many converts refused to recant under torture, and the fact that Christianity never completely died out even in the centuries when Japan was isolated from the rest of the world, is proof of their genuine faith. It is also in keeping with Japanese character. "It is an undoubted fact," comments Sir George Sansom, "that the Japanese people throughout their history have been remarkably ready in peace as in war to suffer as well as to inflict death; and this may account both for the ferocity with which the Japanese Christians were persecuted and the fortitude with which they went to martyrdom."

That year, 1638, marks the withdrawal of Japan from the world. There had been edicts a year or two before which prohibited Japanese from leaving Japan, and ordered Japanese returning from abroad to be put to death. Spanish ships had already been forbidden the country; now the Portuguese were banned. After 1638, only a handful of Dutch were allowed to remain in Japan, and they were strictly confined to a small island off Nagasaki, called Deshima, under humiliating circumstances. Barriers prevented their reaching the mainland. One cargo ship a year was allowed to call at Deshima, and once a year Dutch merchants were formally escorted to Edo to prostrate themselves before the Shogun and present him with gifts. In this way some little knowledge of the western world reached Japan, and vice versa. Otherwise, the ban was complete.

Since the Japanese had no reason to fear missionary activity on the part of Protestant England, it may seem strange that English ships were not allowed to trade at Deshima. England, however, had given up trading with Japan even before 1638, finding it unprofitable. Later in the century, the Japanese apparently became suspicious of the English when they heard that Charles II had married Catherine of Braganza; ignorant as they were of European affairs, they believed that this meant England would be dominated by Portugal. Moreover, at this time England and Holland were intermittently at war with one another, and one can imagine that the Dutch at Deshima did not give the Japanese a very favorable description of their enemies.

By her own choice, Japan thus abandoned the commerce with the western world she had once welcomed. The merchant navy of Ieyasu, unused, rotted away; the dreaded pirate ships ceased to exist. With them went the very real possibility that Japan might have colonized Southeast Asia. Japanese communities already existed in the Philippines and other Pacific islands, and Japanese ships had reached Siam and Cambodia on the one hand, and Mexico on the other. Under Hideyoshi and Ieyasu, Japan had not only the ships and the men, but her people were in an adventurous mood; the European colonizers, coming from half a world away, would have found it hard to compete with her. Now the opportunity was thrown away.

This was even more surprising than the Chinese policy in abandoning their great sea voyages of the early fifteenth century and refusing to build new ships. China had always been a land power, looking inward, and not to the sea. China, moreover, although contemptuous of the barbarians, never absolutely prohibited all foreigners from entering the country. Japan, on the contrary, was a group of islands, her life dependent on the sea, and she had always been open to outside influences. She was favorably situated to build up both a mercantile fleet and an overseas empire. Instead she chose complete isolation, rigidly enforced.

It was a decision based mainly on fear of the subversive influence of Christianity; not so much on the danger of a foreign invasion, although that was possible, as the danger of domestic uprisings inspired or encouraged by this alien faith. The Tokugawa Shoguns were never sure that the powerful feudal lords of western Japan, where Christianity was strongest, would not rebel and bring about a new civil war.

One important result of this policy was to be seen centuries later, when Japanese seclusion came to an end and she faced the modern world. After the 1850's her population, which had remained almost unchanged for several centuries, suddenly increased. Having missed the opportunity to colonize any part of the South Pacific or Australasia, she had no room for this growing population, nor any source of raw materials outside her own islands. The need to find new outlets for her energies, and to make up for the lost opportunities, helps explain Japan's expansionist policies in the late nineteenth and twentieth centuries.

10. *Korea, Bridge*

and Battlefield

A LOOK AT THE MAP will show both the strategic importance
and the vulnerability of the Korean Peninsula. Thrusting
out from the mainland into the Sea of Japan, it is connected
by land with China, Central Asia and the north, while only
a narrow stretch of water divides it from Japan. It can be a
stepping-stone, a barrier or a battleground to its neighbors, and
its land has been occupied and fought over for centuries. It is
vital to both Japan and China that the country should not be
dominated by a hostile power.

The natural boundaries of Korea—the sea, the Yalu River
and the mountains at the neck of the peninsula—are, nevertheless, well defined. Because of this, the Koreans early developed
their own language, culture and way of life. Their traditional

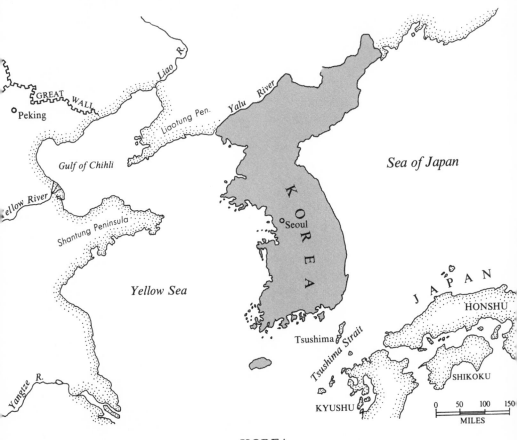

KOREA
LOCATION OF THE PENINSULA

dress—the starched, bulging white coat, full trousers and broad, high-crowned black horsehair hats of the men, and the flowing skirts, with very short blouses, of the women—is distinctive. So is their preference for white, even in working clothes, whereas white in China is used only for mourning. Their cooking differs from that of China and Japan in its emphasis on pickled food and strong pepper seasoning. Their houses, usually clay, with tile roofs, have clay floors covered with heavy brown, oiled paper, and the Koreans are almost the only people in the world (along with the Romans) who used under-the-floor heating from the earliest times.

This Korean identity was preserved in spite of constant, often unwelcome, contact with her neighbors. Prehistoric settlers from Korea, probably of Central Asian origin, helped to people Japan. Chinese culture reached Japan through Korea long before there was any direct contact between these two countries. It was from Korea that the Mongols launched their invasions of Japan in the thirteenth century. It was through Korea that the Japanese tried to invade China in the sixteenth century. Control of Korea was the cause of the Sino-Japanese War in 1894 and the Russo-Japanese War in 1904. This tug of war between outside powers over Korea, increasing in violence with improved communications and modern armaments, has continued into our own time.

Not that Korea was always a battlefield. The ruggedness of her terrain was some protection, and there were long intervals of peace when the Koreans could devote their remarkable talents to art and architecture, sculpture and religion, rather than to war. The magnificent wall-paintings of the Three Kingdoms—Koguryŏ, Paekche and Silla—dating roughly from the fourth to the seventh century, are still to be seen in tombs of that period. The Kings of Silla (668-935) and of Koryŏ (935-1392) built palaces, temples and towers as beautiful as any in China, and their potters produced wares equal if not superior to those of China and Japan, while Buddhist monasteries flourished in the quiet mountains. (Koryŏ is a shortened version of Koguryŏ—a name we have turned into Korea.)

The Mongols destroyed the years of peace. They invaded Korea in 1231, and quickly occupied the entire mainland. They looted towns and cities as they went, carried away thousands of captives, and later imposed almost impossible demands for Korean ships and Korean sailors to man their attempted invasions of Japan. During the fourteenth century, large-scale Japanese pirate raids on Korea added to the country's misery. At times, these raids were so destructive that whole areas of the Korean coast had to be abandoned. This meant not only the loss of the best farmland, but also that the grain paid by farmers in tax could not be shipped by sea; it was either not moved at all, or had to be transported with great difficulty across the mountainous peninsula.

In 1370, two years after the fall of the Mongol Dynasty in China, Korea somewhat reluctantly accepted the suzerainty of the new Ming Dynasty. The royal family of Koryŏ had become puppets of the Mongols, bound to them by marriage and a century of servitude, and there were strong pro-Mongol factions in the government. The country was only saved from civil war when Yi Song-gye, a statesman and general of great talent, known for his victories against the Japanese pirates, rebelled and seized control of the country.

Yi ruled for four years in the name of one of the Koryŏ princes. In 1392, however, he took the throne for himself and founded a new dynasty, which he called Chosen, after the ancient name for Korea, but which is better known as the Yi Dynasty. He made his capital at Kyongsong, or Seoul.

Yi Song-gye's most far-reaching reform was a complete redistribution of land. He abolished all the large tax-free estates, subdividing them and thus increasing the number of inde-

pendent landowners; at the same time he rewarded his own supporters, to whom he gave the name of Merit Subjects, with hereditary grants of land. Although this met with some opposition, and the last King of Koryŏ wept when he saw the old records and land registers being burned (in one huge bonfire, said to have lasted three days), the former landowners had

137

little support outside the now discredited royal family, and their protests were in vain. The new reforms meant that more land was liable to tax; more landowners lived on their own estates rather than as absentees; and those who had received grants of land were more likely to be loyal to the new dynasty. Yi Song-gye wanted all government servants, however humble, to hold some land, but this objective was never fully realized. With each new reign, land had to be allotted to new Merit Subjects, and the lower classes seldom received a share.

The Koreans are a resilient people. In spite of the economic problems inherited by Yi Song-gye, the fifteenth century was a time of prosperity and great cultural activity. Much of this was inspired by China. Korea's written language, her system of examinations and her form of government had all been adopted from China in years past, and now in the Yi Dynasty relations were again very close. As in contemporary Ming China, there was now an enormous literary output: history, philosophy, anthologies of Korean literature, encyclopedias and the Chinese Classics, were among the books printed. These also included a history of Koryŏ, on the Chinese principle that a new dynasty must compile an official history of the preceeding dynasty.

The remarkable thing about these books is that so many of them were printed from movable metal type. The Chinese, who had long since invented paper, and printing from solid blocks, had experimented with movable type, cast in clay. But it was in Korea that metal type, copper and bronze, was invented. The first mention of casting such type was in 1392, over half a century before the supposed invention of printing in Europe, and there may have been earlier castings. In 1403, the third King of the Yi Dynasty lamented that, whereas all edu-

"Sage in Meditation," by Kang Hui-an (1419–1465)
Yi Dynasty, Korea. NATIONAL MUSEUM OF KOREA

cated men, and especially those in government service, should have a wide knowledge of books, printing from ordinary wood-blocks was slow and unsatisfactory. He therefore ordered movable type to be cast in bronze, and ordered every book known in Korea to be printed by that means.

For the next century Korea led the world in printing. So many new and improved fonts of type were cast that there was a shortage of metal for them, and the bronze bells of the old and now disused Buddhist monasteries were melted up to provide it. (Buddhism had fallen out of favor, especially among the upper classes, and was being replaced by Confucianism; monastic lands were confiscated, and monasteries destroyed, by the Yi rulers.) From Korea the use of movable type spread to China and Japan.

Although the Korean spoken language is in no way related to Chinese, most books continued to be written and printed in Chinese. This was despite the fact that the fourth ruler of the Yi line developed a simple, accurate system of phonetic writing, which was officially adopted as the written language of the country in 1446. Onmun, or Vernacular Writing, now known to us as *han'gul*, Korean Letters, is one of the most perfect alphabets in the world. It had everything in its favor except tradition. The uneducated, the lower classes and women, welcomed and used *han'gul*, and a popular literature grew up in the new writing, but the scholars and the men of letters continued to write in Chinese. It was not until the twentieth century that *han'gul* was accepted for general use.

The Koreans were in some ways more conventional than the Chinese. This may have been partly because they had imported Chinese culture; it had not grown among them, and they therefore attached greater importance to preserving it absolutely unchanged. During the Yi Dynasty, Confucianism—that is to say the Neo-Confucianism perfected by Chu Hsi in China in the twelfth century—became the recognized philosophy of the country, not to be questioned, and most officials were extremely orthodox and narrow in their thought.

There was some resistance to this rigid Confucianism. The

teachings of the Chinese scholar Wang Yang-ming (1472-1529) which held that meditation, idealism and individual initiative were more valuable than book-learning, and which, as we have seen, inspired the O Yomei school of philosophy in Japan, were also widely known in Korea. Although frowned upon by the orthodox, Wang Yang-ming's ideas influenced many of the more independent-minded Korean scholars and helped to keep creative thought alive.

The system of examinations was copied exactly from China, with one important difference. In China it was possible for a talented youth to rise from the lower classes through the complicated network of examinations to the very top rank, and to a correspondingly important post in government. In Korea only the Yangban (literally, two groups), the civil and military branches of the upper class, were allowed to take the examinations. There was a sharp division between the Yangban, who were the nobles and landed gentry, and the other three classes, the middle people, the commoners and the low-born; there might be some movement both up and down among these three, but it was virtually impossible for one of them to rise to Yangban class.

The great gulf was, therefore, between the Yangban and the lower classes, not between the Yangban and their rulers. The Kings of Korea never held the exalted position of the Chinese Emperor. There was no question of a Son of Heaven, or divine ruler, the King being scarcely more than first among equals.

Rivalry among the Yangban nobles was one cause of the bitter quarrels which disrupted the Yi Dynasty after the sixteenth century. Political quarrels and factional disputes were nothing new to Korea, but in earlier times these had been brief and usually confined to the capital. The Yi factions now had roots in the countryside among the new hereditary landowners, and in spite of large scale executions and the persecution of whichever happened to be the losing side, they could never be completely destroyed. They would bide their time, recover their losses and fight again.

The origin of these quarrels lay in an irreconcilable difference of opinion about the part to be played in the government by the censors. Like their Chinese counterparts, these men were not censors in a narrow, Puritan sense, but an important branch of the administration. Their position and the amount of influence they exercised affected the whole system of government.

Except for the underlying question of the censors, however, the disputes seldom concerned any politically or ideologically important problem. They centered on dynastic family questions, the succession, minor points of Confucian doctrine and such details as the length of court mourning. They were basically a simple struggle for power. In later years the parties took opposing sides on foreign as well as domestic questions, making it difficult for Korea ever to be united against Japanese or Manchu invasions. From the end of the sixteenth century, the factions hardened into two fixed groups, the Easterners and the Westerners, so-called not because of geography but because their two leaders happened to live in the east and west of the capital, and these persisted throughout the Yi Dynasty. Their fortunes fluctuated and both split into lesser groups, whose names ring strange to us; the Easterners for instance divided into the Northerners and Southerners, the Northerners then into Small Northerners and Great Northerners, and the latter into the Muddy, the Pure, the Skin, the Middle, the Flesh and the Bone Great Northerners.

Meanwhile, disaster came from outside. Hideyoshi, the great Japanese leader, had originally been on friendly terms with Korea, but once he made up his mind to attempt the conquest of China, he was determined that Korea should join forces with him in his campaign. This placed Korea, subservient as she was to China, in an impossible position. The opposing factions disagreed on what to do, some ready to resist, some hoping for a compromise, until Hideyoshi lost patience with them and invaded the peninsula itself. We have seen how his first invasion was defeated by Admiral Yi Sun-sin's control of the seas, how peace negotiations between China and Japan dragged on, and how a second invasion, having met with strong resistance, was withdrawn after Hideyoshi's death.

Although the attempted conquests failed, Japan suffered few adverse effects. Culturally, she even benefited. The Japanese invaders were so delighted by the quality and design of Korean pottery and porcelain that they carried back with them not only vases, bowls and statuettes, but also the artists and potters who had made them. Special kilns were built for these artists, and they introduced improved techniques as well as new designs to Japan; some of the best-known types of Japanese pottery, Satsuma and Imari among them, owe their origin to the Korean influence. Movable metal type for printing was also introduced at this time; the first Japanese book to be printed from movable type appeared in 1596.

The effect of the invasions on Korea, however, was disastrous, leaving the Korean people with a lasting hatred of Japan. The entire country had been laid waste, its villages and towns destroyed, its crops either burned or requisitioned, its bravest men either killed or taking to the hills to form guerrilla bands, its people starving. This would have been bad enough without the looting and vandalism of the Chinese troops who were sent in to help drive back the Japanese. By the time these finally retired, the whole structure of government and society had disintegrated, the records of land ownership and population census were lost, the people were sunk in despair, and the Yi Dynasty entered on a long era of decline.

War-torn Korea would thus have been helpless in the face of the Manchu threat which arose early in the seventeenth century, even if she had not been deeply divided between pro-Ming and pro-Manchu factions. The Manchus found a pretext to invade northern Korea in 1627, when they forced the Korean government to recognize them as the rulers of Manchuria, and again in 1637, when they were preparing for the conquest of China and wanted to secure their flanks. These invasions were brief, but coming so soon after those of Hideyoshi, added to the devastation of Korea.

The collapse of the Ming Dynasty in China was followed

獰猛磨牙欲散逢生東海
老黃公
千今跋扈横行者誰識人中
此顆同
甲午南昌

by the brilliant first centuries of the Ch'ing, or Manchu Dynasty. In Korea, there was no such rebirth. In spite of several major rebellions and all the natural calamities—drought, flood, famine and pestilence—which usually marked the downfall of a government, the Yi Dynasty dragged on through the seventeenth, eighteenth and nineteenth centuries. They were centuries of stagnation, everlasting factional disputes, restrictive government and economic hardship. In the lean years, taxes were raised without any hope of increased production to meet them. Hungry farmers had to borrow seed grain in springtime at such high interest rates that they mortgaged their autumn crops to pay for it, and many gave their land away to anyone who would support them.

There were, of course, intervals of prosperity, when the crops were good and the government less repressive. Naturally industrious and artistic, the Korean people made the best of what they had. After the end of the Manchu invasions, and again during the eighteenth century, there was a revival of the arts and of literature and scholarship. The creative genius of earlier centuries may have been lacking, with literature restricted by the emphasis on the past and on Confucian forms, but the people's talent found expression in music, dancing and impromptu poetry, in simple ink paintings and in handicrafts.

From the seventeenth to the nineteenth centuries, Korea withdrew into herself. Her isolation was not, like that of China and Japan, an attempt to shut out Western influences, which indeed had scarcely touched Korea. It was, rather, to avoid being too closely involved with either of her two great neighbors, which she knew was likely to lead to disaster. At one time, the Koreans apparently even destroyed trees and bushes

"Tiger," Korean Painting, 18th century.
NATIONAL MUSEUM OF KOREA

along their own coast, hoping to make the countryside appear so uninviting that the crews of passing ships would not be tempted to land.

Korea during the eighteenth century was, nevertheless, influenced, although indirectly, by Western ideas. Korean scholars and students often accompanied the annual tribute missions which were sent from Seoul to the imperial court at Peking, and they brought back with them European books and maps, firearms and chiming clocks, as well as new theories of astronomy and mathematics, which they had learned from the Jesuits there.

They also brought back word of a new religion. Christianity was not completely unknown in Korea, since a number of Hideyoshi's soldiers had been Christian converts, but it was only now that the people began to take an interest in what they heard. Buddhism was in disfavor, and Confucianism was a code of ethics rather than a religion. In those years of poverty and hardship it was not surprising that Christianity, with its promise of a better world to come, even if it could offer little help in this world, found an audience.

The remarkable thing about the Christian Church in Korea is that it was well established before a single foreign missionary set foot in the country. Chinese translations of the Bible brought back by the Korean envoys to Peking were read and re-read, and before the end of the eighteenth century there were several thousand self-converted Korean Christians.

In 1786, Christianity was prohibited by the government as being opposed to ancestor worship, and therefore to Confucian morality. During the nineteenth century more and more restrictive measures were put into effect, many converts were martyred, and those who survived were driven to hide their faith. Nevertheless, remote and cut off from the rest of the world although Korea was, and harsh the measures taken against this alien religion, Christianity never altogether died out among her people.

II. *The Great Manchu*

Rulers: K'ang Hsi

and Ch'ien Lung

B Y THE MID-SEVENTEENTH CENTURY, Japan had already
adopted that policy of isolation which was to cut her off
from the rest of the world for over two centuries. Korea, too,
still suffering from the Japanese and Manchu invasions, had
withdrawn into her own shell; withdrawn so successfully that
she became known over the years as the Hermit Kingdom.
China, on the contrary, now ruled by a foreign dynasty, was
entering into a period of expansion, empire-building and brilliant artistic achievement.

The first Emperor of the Ch'ing Dynasty, Shun Chih, was
seven years old when he came to the throne in 1644. His uncle
Dorgun, as Regent, continued to hold supreme power until

his own death in a hunting accident in 1650, and it was he who established the new regime on firm foundations in Peking and North China.

Emperor Shun Chih grew up an ardent Buddhist and was apparently attracted from an early age by the Buddhist ideal of renouncing the world. He may, indeed, have done so, for it is sometimes said that he did not die in 1661 at the age of twenty-four, as officially recorded, but that he retired to become the Abbot of T'ien T'ai Ssu, a temple in the hills west of Peking. Writers of the time spoke of his having followed Buddha's example in throwing away an empire like a worn-out shoe. They quoted Shun Chih himself as telling one of his Ministers that he would be in the crowd which cheered his successor to the throne, and they claimed that when his son and heir later visited T'ien T'ai Ssu, the Abbot did not kneel to him, as any other subject would have done. A gilded mummy of this Abbot, which is still preserved in the temple, is said to bear a strong resemblance to Shun Chih.

Whatever the truth of this story, Shun Chih's successor also came to the throne at the age of seven, with four Ministers appointed as Regents. He reigned for sixty-one years (1661-1722), under the reign title K'ang Hsi, and he was undoubtedly one of the three or four greatest emperors in China's history.

K'ang Hsi took over the government when he was thirteen or fourteen years old, not without opposition from the Regents, and soon faced a desperate situation. Half the country was still in the hands of Ming loyalists or rebel princes—Wu San-kuei among them; Koxinga's heirs held Taiwan and threatened the south coast, while many of K'ang Hsi's own advisers were urging him to abandon south China altogether and hold only the north. The new Emperor, however, refused to consider any such compromise. Within the next fifteen years he succeeded in extending Manchu rule to the whole of China, adding Taiwan as well. He then abolished the system of semi-independent vassal states which had allowed the rebel princes to become so powerful, keeping control of the provinces firmly in his own hands. The fifteen provinces of the Ming

Dynasty were now increased to eighteen by subdividing existing provinces; these eighteen provinces still constitute China proper.

The next threat came from the north, where several Mongol tribes were refusing to recognize K'ang Hsi's authority. It seemed possible that a new Mongol empire might challenge the Manchus, and K'ang Hsi's determination to prevent this led him to push the frontiers of his domain far west into Central Asia, north into outer Mongolia and later into Tibet.

North China has always been subject to invasion; the Manchus themselves were invaders. And there were two reactions to the threat of invasion—one defensive, the other offensive. The first was symbolized by the Great Wall; the Ming emperors, for instance, chose to strengthen their defenses and isolate themselves behind the Wall, a policy which worked well enough as long as they were stronger than any likely combination of enemies. Other dynasties, under the leadership of men such as Han Wu Ti (141-87 B.C.) and T'ang T'ai Tsung (626-649) took the offensive in order to dominate the areas from which China might be threatened, and became, of necessity, empire-builders.

The Ch'ing Dynasty under K'ang Hsi and his immediate successors followed the second course, with the result that during the eighteenth century the Manchus ruled an area greater than that of any other dynasty in the history of China. (The only exception was during the thirteenth century when the Mongol Great Khan, overlord of a vast empire reaching to Russia and the Black Sea, made his capital at Peking.)

While K'ang Hsi thus expanded his empire westward, the Russians were moving east into Siberia and settling colonies along the Amur River valley. Face to face, the two powers clashed in minor skirmishes, and their conflicting claims in the area resulted in the first treaty to be signed between China and a European power. The Treaty of Nerchinsk, in 1689, defined the boundaries between the countries, agreed on the treatment of each other's nationals and allowed for some trade between them. Russian soldiers captured in the fighting were not repatriated, but the Russians were allowed to set up an Orthodox Mission for them and their families in Peking; thus Russia had semi-official links with the Chinese government long before any other western nation was allowed to keep a mission in Peking. The treaty was between equals, not dictated by either side, and the Jesuits at K'ang Hsi's court played a considerable part in negotiating and translating its terms.

The Jesuits were well-treated by the early Manchus. At the end of the seventeenth century there may have been as many as a quarter of a million Christian converts in China. Dorgun, the first Regent, was apparently much impressed by the Jesuits' knowledge of astronomy, their long beards (unusual among the Chinese or Manchus) and their ability to cast cannon. The Chinese had been using gunpowder in firecrackers, especially in religious ceremonies, since the sixth century; they had experimented with its use in explosives since at least the year 1000, and by now they had a variety of firearms and explosive weapons, but these were much less sophisticated than those of the West. K'ang Hsi was so delighted when a new and improved type of cannon was demonstrated for him that he took off his fur-lined robe and presented it then and there to Father Verbiest.

It may seem strange that Christian missionaries were so eager to provide their hosts with firearms. Verbiest even blessed the cannon to be cast, gave each one the name of a Christian Saint and inscribed this in Chinese characters on the barrel of the gun. Expert advice on cannon and cannonballs, and on astronomy, were, however, the two sure ways to win influence at the Chinese or Manchu court. In 1674, Father Verbiest also cast a number of remarkable astronomical instruments, including an armillary sphere, a quadrant, a sextant and a celestial

globe, each about six feet in diameter, and these were set up in an observatory on the City Wall which had originally been built by Kublai Khan in 1296.

K'ang Hsi studied music and science with the Jesuits. He was a man of exceptional intellect and observation, with a quick brain and wide interests; contemporaries speak of his large, penetrating eyes and his ready wit. He was also a man of action. He spent three months of every year in the north country, riding, and hunting with bow and arrow. He traveled widely in China proper, by road and canal, and he was the last of only six emperors in China's history who climbed the Sacred Mountain, T'ai Shan. He combined, as perhaps only T'ang T'ai Tsung (626-649) before him had done, a genius for military operations, administrative ability and a deep interest in culture, especially literature.

K'ang Hsi's character and his long reign help to explain why the Manchu Dynasty lasted almost three hundred years, whereas no other foreign dynasty ever held the whole of China for even a century. With his literary achievements, it is easy to forget that K'ang Hsi was a foreigner. The Great Imperial Chinese Dictionary produced during his reign was compiled under his own supervision; a vast work, including over 40,000 characters, their meanings, tones, and a systematic collection of phrases illustrating their use. It is still the standard work used by students and teachers, and the foundation of all dictionaries in Chinese in European languages. Among his other works were an illustrated encyclopedia, with hundreds of volumes touching on every conceivable subject, a rhyming dictionary and a concordance of literary phrases. The latter enabled a reader who came across an unfamiliar combination of characters to look up exactly where and by whom this had been used, as well as its meaning, and was invaluable in a language like Chinese, which is filled with poetical and historical allusions often quite incomprehensible unless one is familiar with their background.

K'ang Hsi himself composed sixteen short maxims known as the Sacred Edict, which were read out to the people at regular intervals by the officials and the village gentry. They stressed filial piety, the importance of education, of orthodoxy— "Degrade strange religions, in order to exalt the orthodox doctrine"—and of adequate food and clothing—"Give the chief place to husbandry and the culture of the mulberry-tree." (The special importance of the mulberry, which had been cultivated in China since prehistoric times, was that silkworms fed on mulberry leaves. The Chinese kept the trees low by pollarding, thus making it easier to gather the leaves. Production of silk was a major industry; although cotton clothes were in common use by this time, the demand for silk was always great.)

These scholarly works were not the only important literary achievements under the early Manchus. An increasing number of popular plays and novels were written and read by the common people. *The Dream of the Red Chamber*, written about 1757, is the most famous of the novels, partly because it broke away from the traditional retelling of great exploits and legendary heroes to recount the details of life in a single family, presumably that of the author.

Other arts were not far behind. The porcelain works at Ching-te-Chen were restored after having been destroyed during the civil wars, and other potteries were soon in full production. The porcelain of K'ang Hsi's time is technically very fine, and it is highly prized in the West, but there was a certain lack of originality in its design. This remained true in painting, architecture and in life itself. Although the extension of the Chinese empire in the north, and the increasing commerce with European nations by sea had opened a narrow window upon the rest of the world, and the Manchus were never as rigidly isolationist as the Mings, Chinese society and art remained static. Within its limits they had achieved perfection, and their ideal was to equal, not to change, the past. Indeed, the most creative thinkers of the time were those who looked furthest back and studied what was called "Han Learning," the work of writers and philosophers who had lived before the Sung Dynasty— that is, before Chu Hsi's reinterpretation of the Confucian Classics.

Typical of the age was the *Mustard Seed Garden*, a book for painters showing classic examples of every subject they might wish to use. In its pages, the artist could see how different types of mountain landscape, of rocks, trees, houses, bridges and boats, flowers, bamboo, insects and birds, had been treated by earlier masters. There were also delightful little figures— philosophers sipping tea, fishermen, peddlers—to be included in the design. The painter could combine these into a work of his own without even opening the door of his study, although true artists undoubtedly still looked to nature for inspiration, using such manuals to improve their technique and to study details.

K'ang Hsi died in 1722 and was succeeded by one of his sons, a capable but not outstanding ruler, whose twelve-year reign was overshadowed by the long, brilliant careers of his father and of his own son Ch'ien Lung. K'ang Hsi was the first Son of Heaven to reign for sixty years; his grandson Ch'ien Lung, already twenty-five when he came to the throne, not only ruled for sixty years but then abdicated—not wishing, it is said, to remain on the throne longer than his illustrious grandfather—and continued to dominate the court until his death four years later.

It might have been better for China if Ch'ien Lung had not lived quite so long. The eighty-year-old Emperor had lost the keenness, the decisiveness, the energies of his youth, and his judgement failed him on two vital questions. He did not see the corruption growing around him, nor could he imagine that any other country might become strong enough to insist on dealing with the Middle Kingdom as an equal.

But these were only shadows cast ahead by a glorious reign. Ch'ien Lung shared his grandfather's tastes for travel, hunting and an active life, for literature and art. He was a voluminous writer and critic, always ready to compose a poem on the margin of a painting he liked, or a preface for a new book. He carried on K'ang Hsi's work of compiling dictionaries and encyclopedias, although he was a strict censor, suppressing all criticism of the Manchus or of earlier foreign dynasties, and all discussion of the boundaries of China. He employed thousands of writers for almost twenty years (1772-1790) in producing a huge new library of rare and valuable works, 3,450 in all, in over 36,000 volumes. This was called the Four Treasuries because it was divided into Classics, History, Philosophy and Literature. As a by-product, a catalogue of about 10,230 titles, including those copied for the Four Treasuries and others considered for it but rejected, was printed, giving a description and history of each work.

Ch'ien Lung, after almost a century of Manchu rule, inherited a united and prosperous country. During his reign, China's population increased enormously, bearing witness to her continuing prosperity and a high standard of living. Life at the court of Ch'ien Lung was more brilliant, more luxurious and perhaps more formal than at that of K'ang Hsi. For wealth and magnificence, the court of Louis XIV may have been comparable to it, but no European monarch of the time can ever have believed—as Ch'ien Lung certainly did—that the entire civilized world was subject to him and owed him homage. The Chinese Emperor meant what he said when he wrote to George III of England:

"Swaying the wide world . . . our dynasty's majestic virtue has penetrated into every country under Heaven, and Kings of all nations have offered their costly tribute by land and sea. . . . We possess all things. I set no value on objects strange and ingenious, and have no use for your country's manufactures."

The Manchu empire reached its greatest extent under Ch'ien Lung. He defeated the Eleuths, a branch of the western Mongols who had been causing trouble for many years; he conquered Kashgar, Yarkand and the whole area east of the Pamir Mountains, reestablished Manchu suzerainty over Tibet and sent armies across that country into Nepal to drive back the Gurkhas there; he forced the non-Chinese peoples of the south and southwest to accept his authority, and pressed on into Annam and Burma. His relations with these last two countries ended in something of a stalemate, but both sent regular missions with what the Manchus, at least, called tribute.

Ch'ien Lung's first Central Asian campaign precipitated a romantic episode in his life. The wife of a Moslem prince in Turkestan, whose husband had been killed in battle, was taken prisoner and brought back to Peking to be placed in the Emperor's harem. There she became known as the Fragrant Concubine, or the Stranger (K'o) Concubine, and Ch'ien Lung fell deeply in love with her. She, however, could not reconcile herself to her new life. One day during the Moslem New Year, the Emperor found her weeping, overcome with homesickness, and he then ordered a mosque to be built outside the palace wall where she could see it from her window. It was to be surrounded by houses and shops copied exactly from those of her native Turkestan.

But all in vain. The Stranger Concubine continued to mourn, while the Emperor increasingly neglected all else in his efforts to please her. Finally the Empress Dowager, Ch'ien Lung's mother, summoned the girl and reproached her for her

coldness, ordering her to choose either the Emperor's love, or death. "I have chosen death already," she replied, "if only I could be left alone to die! I am guarded night and day." Thereupon, the Empress Dowager dismissed her own attendants and stood guard at the gate while the Stranger Concubine retired and hanged herself from a beam in the Empress' private apartments.

(Moslem services were still held in the little mosque outside the palace walls as late as 1908; the building itself was torn down in 1912 by order of Yüan Shih-k'ai, first President of China, because it overlooked a part of the Forbidden City.)

A strange portrait of the K'o Concubine in Western armor was painted by an Italian Jesuit artist, Father Castiglione (1698-1768). Castiglione also helped design a part of Yüan Ming Yüan, the Old Summer Palace, which was built by Ch'ien Lung some miles outside Peking. This was a Chinese Versailles, modeled on the Trianon; its formal gardens, fountains, obelisks and a maze were completely un-Chinese, yet the roofs rising above the European columns had a definitely Oriental curve, and the trees sculptured on its curious triumphal arch could not have been drawn by a western hand.

The influence of Western art and architecture on China in the eightenth century was, however, far less than that of China on the West. In Europe, especially in France, there was a craze for all things Chinese, and the descriptions and drawings of Chinese buildings and ornaments sent home by Jesuit fathers played a major part in the development of the Rococo style. There were Chinese gardens and Chinese pavilions, Chinese

Emperor Ch'ien Lung giving an audience in the Forbidden City after one of his Central Asian campaigns. HARVARD COLLEGE LIBRARY

screens and Chinese wallpaper, Chinese lacquer and Chinese embroideries. Chinese silks and porcelains were imitated but never equaled in the West. The beautiful monochrome colors typical of eighteenth-century porcelains are familiar to us under the names given them by the enthusiastic Europeans—Peach Bloom; Sang-de-Boeuf, or Ox-blood; Clair-de-Lune, or Moonlight. The habit of drinking tea became so popular that by the middle of the eighteenth century, more tea was being exported from Canton than any other commodity, and people preferred to drink their Chinese tea from Chinese cups, although these had to be made with handles for the export trade. Much of this chinoiserie was more exotic and bizarre than could ever have been found in China, and there was little appreciation of the best in Chinese painting or ceramics. It did, however, awaken an interest in everything Chinese.

Nor was this interest confined to art or frivolities. European philosophers were much impressed by translations of Chinese literature, especially the doctrines of Confucius, and by what they heard of Chinese civilization. They were fascinated by the Jesuits' glowing accounts of the virtues of K'ang Hsi and Ch'ien Lung, and their administration of such a huge country. Voltaire was convinced that the government of the Chinese empire was the best the world had ever known.

This rosy view of China was to suffer a sad decline toward the end of the eighteenth century. The praise of the missionaries gave way to sour accounts of traders who were finding Chinese officials impossible to deal with; attempts to send ambassadors to the court at Peking met with nothing but frustration; and opinion in Europe swung from one extreme to

"Stranger Concubine" of Ch'ien Lung, in Western armor, portrait by the Jesuit Father Castiglione. COLLECTION OF THE NATIONAL PALACE MUSEUM, TAIPEI, TAIWAN, REPUBLIC OF CHINA

another. In the ninetenth century, Chinese culture was either
ignored or treated with contempt.

The missionaries themselves lost much of their influence
during the eighteenth century. The Jesuit Order, which had
played such a major part in establishing Christianity in China,
was formally dissolved by Pope Clement XIV in 1773. This
drastic action was largely due to the enmity of other religious
Orders, and to accusations that they were meddling in European
politics and trade. One of the charges against them was that
before the Rites Controversy was finally settled, they had been
too flexible in allowing their Eastern converts to continue prac-
ticing Confucian ceremonies. However, the Order was restored
in 1814.

The Rites Controversy originated during the reign of K'ang
Hsi, and was primarily concerned with whether Chinese Christians could continue to perform Confucian ceremonies in honor
of their ancestors, as Ricci and the earlier Jesuits had insisted.
There was also some doubt as to whether "God" should be
translated as *T'ien* or "*Shang-ti*," common Chinese words for
Heaven or the Lord of Heaven, or whether some quite different
word, perhaps even a foreign word, must be used to emphasize
the unique nature of the Western God.

There was no question where K'ang Hsi stood. If Christianity were to be acceptable to his people, it must conform to
the ancient ancestral rites of China; and *T'ien* was undoubtedly
the correct translation of God. The Pope, partly influenced by
the growing feeling against the Jesuits among other Catholic
Orders, decided otherwise. Thereupon K'ang Hsi, annoyed by
this attempt on the part of a foreigner to dictate to him, and

even to decide on the meaning of Chinese words, ordered the missionaries either to abide by his decision or to leave China. He, nevertheless, remained on the best of terms with individual Jesuits, and for a time many of these managed to reconcile the Emperor's opinions with their own consciences. In 1742, however, during the reign of Ch'ien Lung, a final edict from the Pope absolutely forbade the priests to allow their converts to observe the ancestral rites, and thus went far toward destroying the Catholic missionary work in China. It also made clear to the rulers of China that in any conflict of loyalty, Chinese Christians were expected to bow to the authority of an alien Church rather than that of their Emperor.

By the end of Ch'ien Lung's reign, corruption had crept into the court and the government. The aging Emperor placed his trust in one Ho Shen, a Manchu of humble origin but quick wit, who first attracted Ch'ien Lung's attention when the latter overheard him explaining a quotation from Confucius to his fellow guards in the palace. His rise thereafter was meteoric. He became Grand Councillor and First Minister, his son married the Emperor's daughter and his henchmen were soon being appointed to important posts throughout the country. During the last years of Ch'ien Lung's life, both before and after he abdicated, Ho Shen came close to ruling China.

In the process, he accumulated an enormous private fortune. After Ch'ien Lung's death his successor brought charges against Ho which described his known assets as something like a billion and a half dollars. He was accused of lèse majesté for having his palace built of imperial cedar wood, an exact copy of the Emperor's own palace; for possessing more pearl necklaces than Ch'ien Lung, and for having a particular pearl, finer than the one in the imperial hat, which he had appropriated from Ch'ien Lung's treasury.

Ho Shen was sentenced to death, being graciously allowed to commit suicide. The new Emperor confiscated what could be found of his treasure, which included vast quantities of gold, jade and precious stones, and items such as thirty-eight European clocks set with jewels, three hundred large rubies, four thousand sapphires, five hundred pairs of ivory and gold chopsticks and at least a thousand sable robes. The washbasins and spittoons in his house were said to be of solid gold. Yet in spite of these great riches, many people at the time believed that Ho Shen had hidden the greater part of his fortune somewhere in the Western Hills outside Peking, and that it has never been found; the lost treasure of Ho Shen has become legendary.

12. Impact of

the Western World

on China

WITH CH'IEN LUNG'S DEATH, the sun had set. Neither Ch'ien Lung's successor, Chia Ching, nor his successor, Tao Kuang, had the ability or the energy of their great ancestors. The weakness of a centralized system of government, with all decisions depending on the Emperor, now became apparent. The old abuses of power crept back; corruption in the government and the army began to be taken for granted. The increase of population during the previous century, which had seemed a sign of prosperity, had not been based on any comparable expansion of production, and it had now outrun the country's resources, resulting in a sharp decrease in the standard of living. Outside China proper, the lack of firm leadership allowed the empire to slip away.

The Manchus were foreigners. They had been accepted and even welcomed in the seventeenth century following the decay of the Ming Dynasty, and the Chinese had taken pride in the achievements of K'ang Hsi and Ch'ien Lung. Now that they had been succeeded by lesser men, however, the Chinese increasingly resented being ruled by an alien people. Secret Societies which were pledged to overthrow the Manchus and their Ch'ing Dynasty now grew increasingly powerful and dangerous to the regime; a major rebellion of the White Lotus Society in 1795 was not put down until 1804, and then only with great loss of life and a scorched-earth policy.

Such rebellions were nothing new. Like living organisms, dynasties grew old and died. This time, however, the downward spiral, already complicated by anti-Manchu feeling, coincided with an age of great progress in the West. The industrial revolution and the age of steam, together with new ideas of liberty and democracy, had brought Europe and America into the modern world, while China, their equal only a century before, remained in a pre-industrial society of horse-drawn carts, sedan chairs and handicrafts. The Chinese were not impressed by the industrial revolution. Unaware that it was, in fact, a revolution, which could transform man's way of life, they still looked upon all western inventions as toys, ingenious but not to be taken seriously.

China was thus quite unprepared for the great extension of sea power and the growth of overseas empires in the nineteenth century. Over the years since the coming of the first Portuguese, they had grown accustomed to foreign ships and foreign traders, but these were restricted to the south coast and had almost no influence on the rest of the country. The influence had been the other way; it had been the Europeans who came in search of Oriental civilization, of Chinese silks, porcelain and tea, and who had been willing to put up with whatever conditions the Chinese imposed on them. Now, without the Chinese realizing it, all this had changed. The Europeans were not only technically in advance of any Asian country, but they were convinced of their own moral superiority. They were determined

*One of the city gates of Peking; painting by William Alexander,
an artist who accompanied Lord Macartney's mission.*

to trade with the Orient on their own terms and, if necessary,
they could and would impose those terms by force.

What were called East India Companies played a great part
in this new age of European expansion. Such companies, for
developing trade with India and East Asia, were established in
the seventeenth and eighteenth centuries by several countries,
among them France, Denmark, Spain and Sweden, but the most
important were the Dutch and the British East India Companies.
Although their original purpose was trade, the Companies were
granted such wide powers under royal charter that in some

166

cases, notably that of the British in India, they actually took over the government of the country. It was their base in India that enabled the British to take the lead in trade with China during the eighteenth and nineteenth centuries.

The first British embassy to the Chinese court was that of Lord Macartney in 1793. The escort provided by Emperor Ch'ien Lung to conduct him to Peking carried banners inscribed, "Ambassadors bearing tribute from the country of England." Ch'ien Lung, however, received the Ambassador courteously and did not insist on the usual ceremony of kowtowing, or prostrating oneself before the Emperor, which was to cause endless trouble for future missions. The Manchus later claimed that Lord Macartney was, in any case, so overcome with awe on entering Ch'ien Lung's presence that his knees gave way, and he fell to the ground, thus actually, if unintentionally kowtowing.

When it came to Macartney's requests to establish a diplomatic mission in Peking, to be allowed to trade at ports other than Canton and generally to enter into the direct relations between sovereign states which seemed normal to England, Ch'ien Lung would not hear of it.

"You, O King," he wrote in his reply to George III, "Impelled by your humble desire to partake of the benefits of our civilization, you have despatched a mission respectfully bearing your memorial. . . . I have perused your memorial; the earnest terms in which it is couched reveal a respectful humility on your part, which is highly praiseworthy. In consideration of the fact that your Ambassador and his deputy have come a long way with your memorial and tribute, I have shown them high favor and allowed them to be introduced into my presence. . . . As to your entreaty to send one of your nationals to be accredited to my Celestial Court and to be in control of your country's trade with China, this request is contrary to all usage of my dynasty and cannot possibly be entertained. . . . Even if your Envoy were able to acquire the rudiments of our civilization, you could not possibly transplant our manners and our customs to your alien soil. . . ."

The gulf of misunderstanding betwen China and the European nations was widening. Neither had the least idea of the other's achievements, civilization or way of life. Europeans were far more ignorant of China in the nineteenth century than they had been in the seventeenth or eighteenth, when Chinese culture had seemed to them so admirable; they now looked upon the Chinese as corrupt and cowardly heathen. The Chinese for their part—and not without reason, at least until the beginning of the nineteenth century—believed themselves to be the largest country in the world, with the highest population; the most enlightened, with the most stable government, and the highest moral code. To them the Western peoples were no different from the tribes of Central Asia, barbarians all, shifting here and there, even changing their names as one tribe absorbed another; there could be no nation among them in any sense comparable to the Middle Kingdom.

In 1816, the second British envoy to Peking, Lord Amherst, was even less successful. After a dispute about whether or not Amherst should kowtow, Emperor Chia Ching refused to receive the party at all and ordered them to leave China immediately. Other countries fared no better, a Russian mission in 1806 being turned back from the gates of Peking when the Ambassador announced that he would not kowtow in the Emperor's presence. Meanwhile, foreign trade by sea was restricted to the single port of Canton, as it had been since 1757. The Peking government's position was that trade was no concern of theirs; if the foreign merchants were dissatisfied with conditions in Canton, they did not have to stay there.

The Chinese could afford to be high-handed. Ever since the Emperor Tiberius forbade Roman women to wear silk because the gold which had to be paid for it was a drain on the Roman economy, the balance of trade between China and the West had been favorable to China. Now an ever-increasing demand for tea, which had become the national drink of England, was added to the demand for silk, porcelain and other luxuries. Europe had little to offer in exchange—a few woolen goods, with some cotton from India—and the balance had to be paid for in silver. Foreign merchants were thus always on the lookout for some commodity the Chinese did want, and would pay for, to redress the balance of trade. In the early nineteenth century they found it in opium.

Opium, a narcotic drug prepared from the juice of the opium poppy, had been known and used as a medicine in China for centuries, but it was not smoked there until after the habit of smoking tobacco spread from the New World to China, by way of the Philippines, in the seventeenth century. The great increase of opium smoking at the beginning of the nineteenth century was partly due to the unsettled times, the decline of good government and the increasing hardships of ordinary life. People smoked opium to forget their troubles, as men in the West might smoke tobacco or drink alcohol. Opium, unfortunately, was not only more harmful to mankind than these, but far more habit-forming.

Most of the opium came from Bengal, where the British East India Company enjoyed a monopoly of opium poppy cultivation. In 1800, only a few thousand chests of opium a year (a chest weighing roughly a hundred and fifty pounds) were being shipped from India to China, but by 1838, the trade had grown to something like forty thousand chests annually. It was entirely illegal. Selling and smoking opium had been prohibited in China since 1729; importing or growing opium was forbidden in 1796. Nevertheless, the habit spread, and the prohibitions against it were seldom enforced, both because opium-smuggling was profitable to all concerned, and because so many government and customs officials were themselves smokers.

China and Britain could well accuse each other of hypocrisy. The opium was shipped in what were called "country ships," independent of the East India Company, so that when China appealed to the Company, the sovereign authority in India, to stop shipments of opium from that country, they could reply that they had no control over cargoes carried by the ships of free and independent merchants. The British, on the other hand, pointed out that the Chinese did not seem to care about the harmful effects of opium-smoking, since they did not enforce their own laws against it, but were only worried by the loss of silver to the smugglers.

It was this situation which led to the so-called Opium Wars of 1839-1842 and 1856-1860. Opium, however, was not the only cause of the wars. The conditions under which the foreign merchants at Canton had to live and do business were frustrating and humiliating. They were not allowed to bring their wives with them, and they were subject to petty restrictions such as not being permitted to ride in sedan chairs. More important, they were strictly confined to an area outside the city walls known as the Thirteen Factories, and they were allowed to trade with only a single group, or guild, of merchants. This guild, known as the Hong, imposed so many duties, taxes and miscellaneous charges on exports that the merchants had very little idea of the true value of the goods or what they might have to pay for them from one week to another. The foreigners were also subject to Chinese criminal law, under which arbitrary arrest, torture and other practices which European nations had come to believe were contrary to the rights of the individual, were common.

The foreign merchants at Canton sought to be allowed to trade at other Chinese ports. They wanted a fixed customs rate instead of miscellaneous duties varying from day to day. They looked for protection from the arbitrary civil and criminal laws of China, and they wanted a representative at Peking who could look after their interests. These all seemed to them, and to their governments, legitimate demands. Within the framework of nineteenth-century thinking, it seemed perfectly reasonable that they should fight for them. Contemporary criticism of the Opium Wars in Britain and America was strong, but it was not directed so much against the principle of using force to obtain trade concessions or political advantages, as against the opium-smuggling trade itself.

In 1839, Emperor Tao Kuang appointed Lin Tze-hsü Imperial Commissioner in Canton, with orders to stamp out the opium trade, without changing the system under which the Canton merchants operated, or yielding to any of their demands.

Commissioner Lin was an honest, patriotic and very stubborn man. His task was, however, impossible, since it meant a head-on collision not only with the merchants but with the British government. Neither the Emperor nor Commissioner Lin had any idea how important the Canton trade as a whole, including the opium trade, had become to the British and Indian trading communities, and to Indian government revenues, nor how strong the British and other Western powers now were. At first, they even seem to have believed that rhubarb, a very minor item in China's trade with the West, was so essential to Europeans as a laxative that if the Chinese refused to export rhubarb they could impose any terms they wished.

Commissioner Lin demanded that the merchants at Canton surrender all the opium in their possession to him; when they refused he held the entire foreign community—several hundred men—prisoners in the Thirteen Factories, without servants and with a minimum of food, until they capitulated. Before they did so, the British Superintendent of Trade in Canton took it upon himself to guarantee that his government would repay British subjects for their losses at a rate of £120 ($600) a chest, thus involving the British government in the quarrel. Twenty thousand, two hundred and ninety-one chests of opium were handed over and publicly destroyed.

Meanwhile, disputes over conditions of trade and the legal jurisdiction of Chinese courts over foreign nationals, became increasingly bitter. The British community was forced out of Canton altogether, and settled on the, then, almost uninhabited island of Hongkong, where Commissioner Lin tried, unsuccessfully, to cut off food supplies from the mainland.

Open warfare broke out in November, 1839 with an encounter between British and Chinese warships. British naval reinforcements arrived in the summer of 1840, and the forts at the river entrance to Canton were stormed and taken, against a brave defense and with heavy casualties among the Chinese. A peace treaty negotiated in 1841 would have ceded the island of Hongkong to Britain, as well as requiring payment of over a million pounds for the opium destroyed. Neither government, however, was satisfied with this. The Emperor refused to ratify the treaty, whereas the British felt that they should have obtained guarantees about future trade; what they really wanted was not so much money or land as a new status for foreigners in China on the basis of equality between sovereign nations, and it was exactly this which the Manchu government could not accept.

The war was soon resumed, and the British not only reoccupied the Canton forts but sailed north along the China coast, taking Amoy and Ningpo. In 1842, they occupied Shanghai, a city of no great importance at that time, and moved up the Yangtze to the outskirts of Nanking.

They were not unopposed. On many occasions the Manchu Bannermen fought desperately and to the death; but they simply did not have either the arms or the organization to withstand the enemy advance. There was also the question of Chinese loyalty to the Manchus. The southern provinces were the heart of opposition to the government, where Secret Societies were working to overthrow the Manchu regime. This helps to explain why British troops, at the time, had the impression that the Chinese were cowards who ran away, while the Manchus were brave men. The Manchus were fighting for their lives and their dynasty. Many Chinese fought with them, but others felt that they were caught in a war between two foreign powers and had no wish to die in defense of the Peking government.

This government was now forced to come to terms. The Treaty of Nanking, signed in August, 1842, provided for Amoy, Foochow, Ningpo and Shanghai, as well as Canton, to be opened to British trade. There was to be a "fair and regular" tariff on imports and exports instead of the arbitrary rates imposed by the Hong at Canton. Within the five ports British subjects were no longer to be judged by Chinese law, but by the law of their own country, a privilege known as extraterritoriality. Hongkong was ceded to Britain, and China agreed to pay an indemnity of twenty million dollars for the opium destroyed and the costs of the war.

This was the first of the Unequal Treaties. Other countries

were quick to take advantage of it. The United States and France negotiated similar treaties in 1844, opening the same ports to their ships and granting extraterritoriality to their nationals; by 1847 Belgium, Sweden and Norway had followed suit.

The basic conflict of interests remained. The foreign merchants assumed that they would be free to expand their trade through the five Treaty Ports, and that they would now be treated by the Chinese as equals. The Chinese, however, remembered the words of Confucius when a disciple asked him how he justified breaking an oath he had given while in the hands of a rebel army: "The spirits do not hear an oath which is forced upon one."

After a few years of uneasy peace, the mounting frustrations and misunderstandings on both sides led to a new outbreak of war in 1856. This was set off by a comparatively minor incident, when Chinese officers boarded the *Arrow*, a ship owned by Chinese but registered in Hongkong and flying the British flag. It is sometimes called the Arrow War. There was such strong opposition in England to the war that the government, defeated on the issue in the House of Commons, dissolved Parliament, appealed to the country and won a new election. French forces, finding a pretext of their own in the murder of a French priest, joined those of Britain. The United States remained neutral, but there was no doubt where her sympathies lay, or that she was ready to take advantage of any new concession won by the allies.

The British and French fleets captured Canton once again and then sailed directly north to Tientsin, the port of Peking, only some seventy miles from the capital. Once they had taken the Taku forts, guarding the approaches to Tientsin, the Emperor (Hsien Feng, son of Tao Kuang, who had succeeded to the throne in 1850) agreed to negotiate with the foreigners, and the Treaties of Tientsin, made with Britain, France, the United States and Russia, were signed in that city in 1858.

These treaties opened a number of new ports in north China and along the Yangtze River to foreign trade. Christians, both

Catholic and Protestant, were to be allowed to preach their religion. The opium trade was legalized, with a regular import duty on the drug, and although this may seem shameful today it was welcomed by some of those most opposed to opium; they believed that if the trade were brought into the open it could be more easily controlled than when the opium was being smuggled into the country. The four foreign powers were to be recognized as equal and sovereign states, and be allowed to maintain representatives in Peking.

Archway in Yüan Ming Yüan, the Old Summer Palace, designed by European Jesuit Fathers. FROM A SET OF ENGRAVINGS MADE BY THE JESUITS ABOUT 1786

Again, this last provision proved too much for the Emperor to accept. When British and French representatives reached Tientsin in 1859, they were denied passage to Peking, and in the fighting which ensued the Anglo-French forces were routed by the defenders of the Taku forts. During this setback the United States navy helped tow boatloads of British marines across the sandbanks into action. This, of course, violated international laws of neutrality, but the Chinese were fortunately unaware of any such laws, while the American commander simply remarked that blood was thicker than water.

Reinforcements arrived the following year, when the forts were stormed and taken for the second time. The Anglo-French forces then moved on toward Peking. Emperor Hsien Feng fled the city and took refuge in a summer residence a hundred miles or so north of Peking, while a truce was negotiated between representatives of his government and those of Britain and France. According to this agreement, the victorious allied armies were to halt some distance outside the capital, while only their leaders entered the city. Meanwhile, however, in spite of the truce, a party of some thirty foreigners was ambushed and captured by Manchu cavalry, and fighting broke out again. Three weeks later, when the invaders finally reached the gates of Peking, their unfortunate comrades were returned to them, some alive, but the majority dead from torture.

The allies were so shocked by the condition of the men who survived, and of the dead, that in retaliation they completely destroyed the Emperor's Summer Palace outside Peking—including that strange Chinese Versailles which had been built by the Jesuit Fathers for Ch'ien Lung. The Palace had already been ransacked by the troops with the help of local villagers, for this was an age when the spoils of war were assumed to belong to the victor, and the men had found themselves in a wonderland of silks and furs, gold, jade, ivory and bronze. The French alone, who were first on the scene, carried away three hundred wagon loads of loot.

There could be no doubt now that the Manchu government must yield to force. The Treaties of Tientsin were ratified and

175

signed again in Peking, and permanent foreign legations were established in that city.

These foreign wars, humiliating although they were, affected only a tiny part of China. From about 1850 to 1870, Peking was far more concerned with a series of peasant-based revolutions which developed into virtual civil wars and led to terrible losses. The most successful and, therefore, most dangerous of these was the Taiping Rebellion, led by an intelligent, fanatical young Cantonese named Hung Hsiu-ch'uan, which broke out in south China about 1850. It attracted wide support among the landless peasants, the unemployed, and all those who blamed the evils of their time on the Peking government. This seemed a familiar pattern: the people were rising to overthrow a dynasty which had run its course. But there was a strange twist to the Taiping Rebellion.

In his youth, Hung Hsiu-ch'uan had had visions which seemed to him incomprehensible, until he read some books which had been given him by a Protestant missionary. He then became convinced that he was the younger brother of Christ, chosen to bring the knowledge of God to his countrymen. His original cause was, thus, purely religious. Soon, however, partly because of the support of one of the Secret Societies, it became a political crusade, a holy war against the Manchus.

The success of the rebellion may have surprised its leader. Discontent was so widespread, the need for reform so great, and after the first Anglo-Chinese war and the humiliating Treaty of Nanking, it was so obvious that China would have to take Western technology into account in the future, that the Taiping movement caught hold in south China and spread like fire. By 1853, the rebels had occupied the Yangtze Valley and captured Nanking, where they massacred the entire Manchu population. Hung Hsiu-ch'uan thereupon proclaimed a new dynasty, the Taiping, or Great Peace, with himself as its Heavenly King and Nanking as its capital. For over ten years his armies extended their conquests throughout the country, capturing major cities in sixteen provinces, until at one time they were less than a hundred miles from Peking itself. It seemed more than likely that the decadent Manchu dynasty would be driven out, to be replaced by this new, native dynasty.

Conservative Chinese, however, and the gentry, seeing a "Christian" rebellion as a threat not only to the existing government but to the entire fabric of Chinese-Confucian society, strongly supported the Manchus. A leading Chinese statesman, Tseng Kuo-fan, and other Chinese officials organized a volunteer force which played a major part in suppressing the rebellion. The Heavenly King's own fanaticism and his alien doctrines lost him the popular support which was essential to his cause. Christian missionaries, too, found it impossible to support a man who claimed to be the Brother of Christ.

Ironically, the very same foreign powers who had been intermittently at war with China for over twenty years, now contributed to the defeat of the Taipings. At first, many foreigners had favored the rebellion, thinking that men who practiced even such a peculiar form of Christianity might be less hostile to the West than the Manchus. By 1860, however, they had realized that the Taipings were not more moderate but more intolerant than the Manchus. Moreover, having at last signed a treaty with the Manchu government which gave them what they wanted, it was to their interest to keep that government on the throne.

Foreigners in Shanghai, accordingly, raised an army of their own under the leadership of Frederick Ward, an American, which proved so successful against the Taipings that it was nicknamed the Ever-Victorious Army. After Ward's death in action, the British Army lent Major Charles George Gordon to command this force, consisting largely of Chinese troops with foreign officers. The Ever-Victorious Army and the Chinese volunteers under Tseng Kuo-fan cooperated in driving the Taipings out from one stronghold after another, until only Nanking was left to them. The Heavenly King himself died in Nanking in the summer of 1864, and a few weeks later his capital fell to the army of Tseng Kuo-fan.

Although foreign troops took no part in the final siege, they undoubtedly hastened the downfall of the Taipings. Major

Gordon received the Order of the Yellow Riding-jacket from a grateful Peking government, and long after he had left China he was known as Chinese Gordon. (Twenty years later, in 1885, General Gordon—as he then was—was murdered in Khartoum by followers of the fanatical Sudanese leader known as the Mahdi, and he is now best remembered as Gordon of Khartoum.)

13. *The Years of Seclusion, and the Reopening of Japan*

WHILE CHINA in the early nineteenth century was increasingly exposed to the pressure of foreign interests, Japan maintained her isolation. For two and a half centuries, under the rule of the Tokugawa Shoguns, she was free from foreign or domestic wars. She was, however, almost entirely cut off from the Western world, although some "Dutch learning" did trickle in from the settlement at Deshima. No Europeans except those few Dutchmen were allowed to set foot in Japan, nor were Japanese permitted to leave the country. Trade with China continued, but it was limited by quota, and the Chinese merchants were also confined to Nagasaki.

Such isolation, coinciding as it did with the industrial revolution in the West, inevitably caused Japan to fall behind technologically. Whereas in the sixteenth century Japan had been on much the same level as the European countries, the years of seclusion held her static and unchanging while the West moved far ahead. She was quite unprepared to face the modern world. Within its own limits, however, the country prospered, while the arts flourished and took on new vitality.

Japan's society was conservative and strongly Confucian, and although the sharp division between different classes had become somewhat blurred over the centuries, the great gulf between the Samurai and the other three classes remained. The Samurai enjoyed unique rights and privileges, even to the power of death over anyone of a lower class who failed to behave toward them in the expected manner (a rude man is described as being "an other than expected fellow"), but they were also bound to observe higher standards of conduct than other men. The code of the warrior class, which is now known as Bushido, demanded absolute loyalty to one's master, courage, honor, self-control and chivalry toward the weak and helpless. Such principles were obviously not observed by all Samurai, but the ideal was not lost sight of even in the twentieth century.

The most famous example of this heroic ideal is the story of the Forty-seven Ronin. At the court of the Shogun in Edo, in 1702, Asano, the lord of Ako, was so provoked by the insults of a nobleman named Kira that he lifted his sword and struck him in the face. Although Kira was only slightly wounded, it was a capital offense to draw one's sword within the palace, and Asano was ordered to commit hara-kiri, the honorable but extremely painful form of suicide by disemboweling.

Because of this, Asano's forty-seven retainers became Ronin, or wave-men, so called because they did not owe allegiance to any one lord but were tossed hither and yon like waves. The forty-seven scattered, some in disguise, some working at menial tasks, some drinking and gambling, giving the appearance of having quite forgotten their dead master. Secretly, however, they plotted their revenge. After a year or more had passed, Kira, believing that he had nothing to fear, relaxed his guard a little and the forty-seven were able to force their way into his house one winter night during a snowstorm, and overpower his retainers. When Kira refused to commit hara-kiri, as an honorable man should have done, they beheaded him with Asano's own sword.

The forty-seven then placed Kira's head upon the tomb of their lord, Asano, and gave themselves up to the authorities. Their revenge was acclaimed by all as just, right and according to the code of the Samurai. All forty-seven of the Ronin were, nevertheless, sentenced to commit hara-kiri, which was the penalty for having taken the law into their own hands, and they did so without question. They were buried beside their former master, where their tombs became a great center of pilgrimage and prayer, and their memory has influenced Japanese thought down to our own time. As recently as the 1930's, on the eve of the second World War, a detailed account of their heroic action used to be read out to army units every year on the anniversary of their deaths.

The code of the Samurai led them to despise money and the men who lived by money. Yet as the economy became increasingly based on money, they could not do without it, and they were forced to borrow. Their mounting debts led to a paradoxical situation where the elite of the country, the Daimyo and the warrior class, were reduced to living on the bare necessities of life, while the despised merchant class grew rich. Families like the Mitsui, which were to build up industrial and financial empires in the late nineteenth and twentieth centuries, laid the foundation for their success during this period.

At the same time, the standards of life and education among all classes were improving. In early Tokugawa times, the nobles and the Samurai had been inclined to treat the peasants as low-grade workers whose only purpose in life was to provide food for themselves and others, and official edicts concerning agriculture would begin, "Since peasants are stupid people, without sense or forethought . . ." and go on to order them to work early in the morning and late at night, to eat coarse grains instead of rice, and not to indulge in luxuries such as tea or tobacco. Now, at last, they were credited with some intelligence and with skills of their own. Scientific treatises on farming and other subjects of interest to the non-military classes were available to them; educational opportunities, although still very limited, were increasing—and, perhaps most important of all, they were gaining self-respect in relation to other classes.

The prosperity of the merchants and the money-lenders at this time had considerable influence upon Japanese culture. Whereas the aristocracy and Samurai were always seeking inspiration in the past, and were contemptuous of any art which might be called popular, the new capitalists had no such inhibitions. They wanted amusement, color, novelty. Under their patronage, the arts became popular and lively. The Kabuki theater, less rigid in form than the classical No dance, developed at this time and enjoyed an immediate success. So did the puppet theater, in which wooden dolls, some three feet high, were manipulated from behind by men in black robes and hoods; these black-robed figures, making no attempt to be invisible, only seem to add to the realism, and the dolls took on an extraordinary life of their own. Many contemporary plays were written especially for the puppets.

These popular arts reflected a general atmosphere of gaiety, extravagance and a constant search for pleasure which was transforming the life of the cities. It was not only the theater. Shops and bazaars catered to the new demand for frivolities such as fans, jewelry, lacquer and cloisonné work; strolling players and jugglers entertained the crowds; and in Edo, at least, there was an entire section, known as the Nightless City, set aside for courtesans and their customers. This light-hearted new world was called Ukiyo, the Floating World, because it was made up of passing things, things of the moment. Although frowned

"Women making Wood-block Prints," wood-block print by Utamaro

upon and even forbidden to the upper classes, the Floating
World was by no means vulgar or tasteless; moreover its art
was a truly native art, an expression of the innate Japanese
feeling for color and design and their appreciation of beauty
even in the most inexpensive and perishable things.

The effect on painting was important. A school called the
Ukiyo-e, or Floating World Picture, although descended from
the classic schools of Kano and Tosa, increasingly reflected
popular taste. Hokusai (1760-1849) and other contemporary

*"The Great Wave at Kanagawa," wood-block print
by Hokusai.* THE METROPOLITAN MUSEUM OF ART
(HOWARD MANSFIELD COLLECTION, ROGERS FUND, 1936)

artists, Hiroshige and Utamaro among them, began reproducing
their work in wood-block prints which were sold for a penny
or less. Even the poorest classes could afford these prints; they
were collected and enjoyed by men who could never have
bought—probably never even have seen—original paintings by
good artists. The prints varied, of course, in quality, but the
best are masterpieces in their own style. They also give an
invaluable picture of life at that time. The Floating World of
actors, courtesans and their serving maids, of wrestlers, jugglers
and strolling musicians, of street festivals and processions, comes
alive in brilliant color, and there are also quiet sketches of
peasants at work, pilgrims with lantern and staff, and landscapes.

These print-makers may have gained a new idea of perspec-
tive from seeing western paintings brought in by the Dutch
merchants at Deshima, but it did not affect their completely
Japanese style of drawing. Hokusai was, perhaps, the greatest of
them. He left behind him thousands of drawings, paintings and
illustrations which have become world famous. Yet he was a
modest man; before he died at eighty-nine he remarked that,
although he had gathered some grains of wisdom from the vast
shore of life, if only he had lived to be a hundred he might
have learned to draw.

Even before Japan was opened to the West in 1854, many
Ukiyo-e prints, colorful and cheap, had been carried back to
Europe by the Dutch and become popular there. European
artists of the nineteenth century were so intrigued by the prints
that many painters, Whistler and the Impressionists among
them, experimented with painting in the Japanese style.

Commodore Perry, who anchored his four ships off Edo

in 1853 and insisted on delivering a letter from the President of the United States to the Emperor of Japan, was not the first westerner to try to break down Japan's isolation. A Russian naval officer returned some shipwrecked Japanese sailors to Japan in 1792, hoping to establish friendly relations, and in 1804, a Russian embassy visited Japan for the same purpose, without success. In 1837 and again in 1846 American ships tried to negotiate with the Japanese authorities and were driven off. The difference in 1853 was that Commodore Perry was ready to use force to get what he wanted: an agreement that Japanese ports should be open to American shipping, and that shipwrecked American sailors would be given safe-conduct out of the country.

The Japanese were well aware of the danger they faced. The Anglo-Chinese war of 1838-42 had shown that their great continental neighbor, apparently so powerful, had not withstood the forces of the West. China had been forced to open her ports, allowing Europeans to live and trade there. Was it likely that Japan could resist them? One school of thought maintained that she could; that the courage and faith of the Japanese Samurai were proof against any enemy, however strong, while Japan had the added advantage of being an island country. The more realistic statesmen argued that their medieval weapons were no match for the modern armaments of the Americans, and that, however much they disliked the foreigners, they must come to terms with them.

Instead of asking for an immediate decision, Perry promised to come back a few months later. It was, nevertheless, clear to everyone that if on his return he did not get a satisfactory answer to the proposals he had made, he would then attempt a landing in force. Meanwhile, the Shogun had time to consult the more powerful feudal lords, as well as Confucian scholars and philosophers. The realists won the day and it was decided to accept Commodore Perry's terms.

The first treaty, signed in 1854, agreed that shipwrecked American sailors should be well treated and repatriated, while American ships would be allowed to refuel and take on provisions at two Japanese ports, Shimoda and Hakodate. This was an important concession at that time, when ships were just beginning to use steam, since Japan lay on the direct route from the United States to the Treaty Ports newly opened in China. Whereas sailing ships, if they had food and water enough, could make long voyages without calling at any port, the steamers must refuel.

An American Consul was to be allowed to live in Shimoda to look after American interests in Japan. It was the thin end of the wedge. Britain obtained a similar treaty in the same year; the Russians followed suit in 1855, and the Dutch in 1856. The Russians added Nagasaki to the ports which were to be open to Europeans. They also persuaded the Japanese to grant them extraterritoriality, and under the "most-favored-nation" principle, other countries received the same right. (The Western countries insisted on having what was called a "most-favored-nation" clause in their treaties with China and Japan. This guaranteed that any right or privilege granted to one nation would be extended to all other nations which already had treaties.)

These agreements with Japan were not commercial treaties; they placed Japan under no obligation to trade with the foreigners. Within a few years, however, thanks largely to the patience and tact of Townsend Harris, the first American appointed to reside in Japan, commercial treaties were also negotiated with the United States, Britain and other European countries.

The treaties were signed by the Shogun, the actual ruler of the country, whose government and headquarters were at Edo. The Emperor and his court at Kyoto remained resolutely isolationist and anti-foreign and refused to sanction the treaties, a situation which caused some confusion among the foreigners. They often believed that the Shogun and his government at Edo were acting in bad faith when they were, in fact, trying to obtain the Emperor's approval of agreements they had already signed.

The settlement of foreign Consuls in the country led to

violent incidents, and several of the hated foreigners, Russian, British and American, were assassinated in the streets, or even in their own Legations. There was little doubt that these murders were politically inspired; the battle-cry of the assassins was "Revere the Emperor! Expel the foreigner!"

In 1863, a British merchant was murdered by men of the Satsuma clan. The British demanded compensation, and when this was refused their ships bombarded the Satsuma stronghold at Kagoshima. The result was surprising. The lord of Satsuma was so impressed by the British sea-power that, having surrendered, he set about establishing friendly relations with the foreigners, and somewhat later he invited the British admiral to stay with him; it was partly because of this that the modern Japanese navy was modeled on that of Britain. One of the young Satsuma nobles who fought in the battle of Kagoshima was among those sent to England for naval training; forty years later, as Admiral Count Togo, it was he who routed the Russian fleet at the battle of Tsushima in 1905.

It was clear that there was no hope of expelling the foreigner. The other half of the slogan, "Revere the Emperor!" now took on new importance, and there was a powerful movement to restore the government, which had been usurped by a series of Shogunates since the twelfth century, to the imperial line. There was also a move to abolish Dual Shinto, a long established compromise between the native Shinto faith and Buddhism, and return to the original, Pure Shinto, which stressed the divine ancestry of the Japanese Emperor.

Here the Tokugawa Shoguns' adoption of Confucianism as a moral code on which to base their rule reacted against them. Loyalty to the sovereign is important in the Confucian ethic. Students of Confucian thought could not ignore the fact that the Shoguns had usurped power, and most Confucian scholars favored a return to the monarchy.

The foreign treaties worked to the advantage of the Emperor. Although responsible statesmen realized that there had been no choice but to give in to Perry, it had been a great blow to their pride. The Tokugawa Shoguns were held responsible not only for having signed the treaties but for having allowed the country to become so defenseless that they could not meet an enemy on equal terms. The Emperor himself, never having held power, was obviously not to blame.

Things came to a head when four southwestern clans, among them Satsuma and Choshu, rebelled against the Shoguns in the name of the Emperor. A brief civil war resulted in the overthrow of the last Tokugawa Shogun in 1868, with the restoration of full power to the sovereign; this was called the Meiji Restoration because the Emperor now took the reign-name of Meiji, or Enlightened Rule. The court moved from Kyoto to Edo, now renamed Tokyo, or the Eastern Capital. Fortunately for Japan, the newly restored Emperor, although only sixteen at the time, was a man of character and ability. With the help of advisers from the four clans which had brought him to power, he was able to push Japan into the modern world within his lifetime.

Far from resisting foreign influence, Emperor Meiji and his ministers threw themselves headlong into reorganizing the country along foreign lines. Their success was phenomenal. The army and navy, with the help of foreign advisers, were transformed into modern fighting forces; the navy was modeled on that of Britain, the army on that of Germany. The army even took in conscripts, which was completely contrary to the old Samurai ideals. Modern industrial techniques and modern ideas of banking and commerce were enthusiastically adopted. Foreign trade was encouraged. Railroads were pushed out into areas where not even a road had run before; shipyards, mines, factories and textile mills were set up and financed by the government before being handed over to private companies as going concerns.

All this was not achieved without hardship. Unlike China, the Japanese government wisely decided that to finance these new ventures with foreign loans would be to place themselves dangerously in debt to other countries, and they borrowed as little capital as possible. The terms of the treaties Japan had signed did not allow her to place heavy duties on foreign imports. Money had to be raised from the land itself, and an annual land tax, payable in cash, imposed a heavy burden on the farmers. Within the next generation or two, however, the poorer classes also began to benefit from modern techniques, the abolition of the rigid class system, education for their children, and the greater opportunities open to them all. Primary education was made compulsory early in Meiji's reign, and illiteracy soon ceased to be a problem in Japan.

There were some who thought the changes went too far too fast. Many Samurai, although loyal supporters of the Emperor, believed that the security of the country depended on an elite warrior class; they were dismayed by the organization of the new army and by other drastic reforms. Their opposition culminated in the Satsuma Rebellion of 1877, led by Saigo Takamori, a man who had done much to bring about the Meiji Restoration, but who now felt that the government's policy had become dangerously radical. Saigo, gallant, chivalrous, idealistic, represented all that was best in the warrior class. But he was struggling against the tide. After several months of bitter fighting, the rebellion was suppressed, partly by the very conscript armies so despised by the Samurai, and Saigo died in battle.

Meanwhile, a minor revolution in transport had taken place about 1868 with the introduction of the Jinrikisha (literally, man-power-carriage). The Jinrikisha is a chair on wheels, pulled by a man running between two long shafts; it is well balanced and there is no great strain involved when it is pulled by an adult on level ground. Its invention is variously credited either to an ailing Kyoto nobleman, or an American missionary with an invalid wife. Be that as it may, the Jinrikisha was an imme-

"American Tourists, Nagasaki" (*or "American Lady with Naval Officer"*), *Japanese wood-block print.* PRINTS DIVISION, THE NEW YORK PUBLIC LIBRARY, ASTOR, LENOX AND TILDEN FOUNDATIONS

亞墨利加人

diate success, and by the end of the nineteenth century, over forty thousand such vehicles were licensed in Tokyo alone. The Jinrikisha was quickly adopted throughout Asia and, although it has now been largely replaced by motor transport, variations of the original model are still in use.

Emperor Meiji lived until 1912. During his lifetime, and with his approval, Japan adopted constitutional representative forms of government. The Constitution provided for a Cabinet, Ministers of State, and a two-house Parliament, the Lower House to be made up of elected members. Although it was stressed that these concessions were freely granted by a benevolent Emperor, and did not belong to the people by right, they were undoubtedly a step towards constitutional monarchy and popular government.

Long before Meiji's death, Japan had become a world power. The unequal treaties had been replaced by agreements between equals, extraterritoriality had been abolished, and Japan had been victorious in two wars against countries far larger and apparently more powerful than herself.

The contrast with China is striking. China and Japan had seemed equally isolated, equally weak, equally unprepared to face the modern world. In both countries the foreign challenge came at a time when the ruling house was at a low ebb; the Manchu Dynasty in China, now weak and corrupt, had apparently run its course, while in Japan the Tokugawa Shogunate was also in decline.

There were, however, important differences. The Japanese had never believed themselves to be the only civilized country in the world, nor their Emperor to be the ruler of All Under Heaven. They had always been willing to learn from others— to adopt Chinese philosophy, Indian religion, Korean sculpture —to make it their own and often in so doing to improve on the original. Now they were willing, if they must come into contact with European civilization, to use it to their own advantage. Such flexibility was alien to the very nature of Chinese society, based as it was on the conviction that they had already achieved perfection.

Japan is a comparatively small country. A strong government could concentrate its resources, modernize its communications and force its people into a new mold far more easily than China, almost a continent in itself, could do. The Japanese, moreover, are of a curious disposition, interested in everything new and different. The morning after Commodore Perry's ships cast anchor in Japanese waters, they were surrounded by small boats filled with sightseers, among them artists eagerly making sketches of these strange creatures who had appeared from nowhere. Within a few days, wood-block prints of the ships and their crews, with the red hair and large noses supposed to be typical of all western barbarians, were on sale in Edo shops.

An even more important difference was that at this crucial time, the rulers of China were foreigners. The Manchu Emperor could not, as Emperor Meiji had done, overthrow the existing government and take the lead in reforming his country, appealing to native patriotism and tradition, for he himself was an alien, and any such reformation would almost certainly be directed against his own dynasty. In 1898, Emperor Kuang Hsu did attempt to introduce reforms within the framework of the Manchu Dynasty, but in this he failed. It was not surprising, therefore, that the Manchus fought to the bitter end against the modern world, the foreigners and foreign ways, and even against internal reforms; they knew that their own existence was at stake.

14. The Sino-

Japanese War

THE THIRTY YEARS between the crises of the mid-nineteenth century, the Anglo-French Wars and the Taiping Rebellion, and the even more traumatic and tragic events of 1894 and 1900 seemed to bring little change within China. In fact, the Manchu Dynasty was coming to an end, with or without foreign pressure.

The Taiping Rebellion had been only one of many. The Miao tribes in western Kweichou Province were in constant rebellion from 1854 to 1873. There were several large-scale Moslem risings; one in Yunnan Province in the southwest, where the rebels set up an independent Moslem state which lasted for over twelve years, and others in remote Kansu Province and

Central Asia. Scattered groups of defeated Taipings joined forces with other dissidents in central China between the Huai and Yellow Rivers; these, and the Moslem rebellions, were finally crushed in 1873. The year 1873, in fact, saw the end of the great rebellions, with the Ch'ing Dynasty once more apparently sovereign in China. Their success had, however, been won by wholesale slaughter, by laying waste entire provinces and by further weakening the economy and the central authority. Provincial rulers who had helped put down the rebels were now powerful in their own right and capable of acting independently.

In Peking, meanwhile, Emperor Hsien Feng, who had died in 1861, was succeeded by a child, Emperor T'ung Chih; he had scarcely come to manhood before he, too, died, to be succeeded by another infant. And throughout the country, natural disasters added to the misery of the people; thousands died or were made homeless by drought in the northern provinces and floods in the south.

Foreign barbarians were nibbling away at the edge of the Manchu empire. The number of Treaty Ports open to traders was increased with every new agreement signed. Between 1863 and 1884, France gradually annexed Cambodia and most of the Indochinese peninsula. Britain completed the conquest of Burma in 1886. Russia had taken over parts of Central Asia which had long been tributary to China, and stood ready to move further east and south whenever an opportunity presented itself. Japan had occupied islands in the Pacific both north and south of her own archipelago, including the Ryukus, near Taiwan and within the Chinese sphere of influence.

In the face of all this, the Manchu Dynasty, although shaken, survived. It was still supported by the majority of intellectual, patriotic Chinese, men like Li Hung-chang and Tseng Kuo-fan, who had led the resistance against the Taiping rebels—men who were convinced that the preservation of the existing order was essential if the values of Confucius and of China's long history were not to be swept away. What they had seen of the foreigners only confirmed their feeling that these were barbarians whose coming would destroy Chinese civilization. They were, therefore, determined to make as few changes as possible, and to keep the flood of Western learning and science which threatened to overwhelm them down to a trickle.

Many people did recognize the need for reform. Li Hung-chang pointed out as early as the 1860's that if China did not make use of foreign inventions, then not only the West but Japan would take advantage of her weakness. Even these men, however, believed that they could borrow foreign techniques, means of communication, weapons, and so forth, while maintaining Chinese ways of thought and Confucian values unchanged. Known as Self-strengthening, this was the policy generally followed during the last thirty years of the nineteenth century. It was, unfortunately, based on a complete misunderstanding of the nature of the revolution which had taken place in the West. Its advocates did not realize that Western science and technology were not simply a matter of mechanical skills but had grown in the soil of a totally different society. To them the sophisticated modern armaments, the locomotives, the mining equipment, were no different from the clocks and other mechanical curiosities of the sevententh century; wind them up and they must go.

During these thirty years, Chinese Legations were opened in several European countries and the United States, and young Chinese were sent abroad to study. There were never many of these students who "drank foreign ink," as the saying was, but on their return they exercised considerable influence on the government. With the help of foreign advisers, a start was made towards building a modern navy, railroads, factories and a few technical schools where modern science and industry were taught. These were all government projects, involving no competition, free enterprise or capitalists. They were also largely financed by foreign loans, thus further mortgaging the future of China to foreign banks.

The vacuum created by China's lack of comprehension of what was involved in a modern state, together with the atrophy and corruption of its own governmental machine, now led to the establishment of unique institutions: governmental bodies set up and operated by foreigners to serve the Chinese government. The most important of these was the Imperial Maritime Customs Service. This was born in Shanghai during the Taiping Rebellion, when civil war made it impossible for the government to collect the duties owing to them from foreign trade. The foreigners, therefore, collected the duty themselves and handed it over to the Chinese. This system proved so satisfactory to both sides that it was extended to other Treaty Ports and soon became a nationwide service.

The China Customs was the first modern institution in China. From collecting Customs duties, its activities grew to include almost everything concerned with navigation and coastal trade; charting rivers and harbors, building lighthouses and installing buoys to mark the shipping routes, issuing statistics on imports and exports, tides, weather and so forth.

The foreigners also set up a Postal Service, and a Salt Revenue Administration, the latter to collect the important salt taxes. These three bodies provided the Chinese government with its major and only reliable sources of income, and they also satisfied the foreign powers, since this income could be used as backing for their loans. They performed good service for China throughout war and revolution. Although they employed large Chinese staffs, the higher officials in all these organizations were Westerners, mostly British in the Customs, and French in the Postal Service; they were honest, competent men, loyal to the government they served at a time when almost no Chinese would have been able or willing to fill such positions.

Trade did not expand as rapidly as the foreign merchants had hoped. The dream of hundreds of millions of customers remained a dream. The Treaty Ports, however, especially Shanghai, prospered and grew into flourishing cities with large populations, both Chinese and foreign. Because, under extraterritoriality, the foreigners lived by their own laws and were judged by their own courts, it was easier if they all lived in the same area; as a result, foreign Concessions, policed by Western nationals, with Western-style buildings, Western clubs and an altogether European way of life, grew up in Shanghai, Tientsin and other ports.

In the early days of the Treaty Ports, the segregation of foreigners had been a sensible and convenient system for controlling a few hundred people. This was how the Chinese themselves had organized it at Canton. Through the turbulent years at the end of the nineteenth and beginning of the twentieth century, however, the foreign population of the Treaty Ports grew to several hundred thousand, while remaining independent of Chinese law and free of Chinese tax. The International Settlement and French Concession at Shanghai for instance, although Chinese territory, were entirely governed by foreigners; the original idea of extraterritoriality had thus become an encroachment on China's sovereignty.

The Treaties of Tientsin allowed Christian missionaries to preach anywhere in China. Roman Catholics and Protestants alike, especially the French and British, followed somewhat later by the Americans, took advantage of this to travel and to found Missions throughout the country. They built schools, practiced and taught medicine, translated the Bible and a few Western histories and textbooks into Chinese, and carried Western ideas, in general, into the inland provinces. They had to learn Chinese, as the Treaty Port merchants often did not, and many of the earliest Chinese dictionaries, grammars and so forth were compiled by the missionaries.

Most of these were dedicated men who devoted their lives to fighting disease, famine, poverty and illiteracy in areas where the merchants and the diplomats did not, and at this time could not, go. Yet they were not only foreigners, their teaching was alien to Chinese tradition. It was now agreed that it was impossible to become a Christian while remaining a Confucian, and there was widespread, sometimes violent, opposition to the presence of the missionaries. They made genuine converts, but there were many others scornfully known as Rice Christians because they paid lip service to the foreign religion for the advantages it brought them.

These thirty years of comparative peace were marked by

198

the increasing power of the Empress Dowager Tzu Hsi, a remarkable woman, ambitious and unscrupulous, with an extraordinary talent for manipulating men and events to her own advantage. For half a century, whoever might be called Emperor, she ruled China. Her strength of character probably enabled the Manchu Dynasty to survive longer than it would otherwise have done. In the end, however, she was a major cause of its downfall and of the chaos which followed. Without her blind hatred of foreigners, and her determination to resist even the most obvious internal reforms, China might have been spared the Boxer Rebellion and might have been able to introduce moderate reforms before it was too late. The Chinese saying, "Disaster follows the crowing of a hen," proved right.

Tzu Hsi, born in 1835, belonged to one of the ancient Manchu clans. She was among those chosen as senior concubines of the Emperor Hsien Feng, and she soon became his favorite; in 1856 she gave birth to his only son and heir. After Hsien Feng's death in 1861 she and the Emperor's widow became co-Regents for this infant son, T'ung Chih, and although they both enjoyed the rank of Empress Dowager there was no doubt from the beginning who was in command.

Tzu Hsi inherited many of the qualities of the early Manchu rulers. As a woman, however, born at a time when the dynasty was already in decline, she had little scope for such qualities and she turned her talents instead to intrigue and the pursuit of power and wealth. She played one leader or one faction off against another with great skill, and she had a sixth sense which warned her of any possible opposition. The number of people who died of strange illnesses when their existence became inconvenient to her is suspiciously large.

In foreign affairs she consistently favored resistance to the barbarians. She was misinformed, or blind, as to how strong they were. In 1860, she urged Hsien Feng to stay in Peking, believing that his mere presence there would so awe the foreigners that they would retreat. She agreed with her advisers on the need to build up a strong modern army and navy, and perhaps even convinced herself that this was being done. Yet

when the funds raised for the navy were largely diverted by
her favorite eunuch, Li Lien-ying, into building a magnificent
Summer Palace for herself, she was delighted. Pretending to
justify the use of naval funds for this purpose, she had a marble
pavilion built in the shape of a boat at the edge of a lake in
this new Summer Palace.

In later years the Old Buddha, as she was affectionately

known to her people, spent much of her time at the Summer Palace. She loved the theater, fancy dress and every form of entertainment, and she could enjoy such pleasures more readily outside the capital than she could in the Forbidden City itself. Even in her years of supposed retirement, however (1889 to 1898), she kept in close touch with palace affairs, ready to step in at any moment if things did not go as she wished.

The Manchus had not forgotten the part played by eunuchs in the downfall of the Ming Dynasty. Censors, statesmen and the Empress herself were unanimous in agreeing that they should not hold power. Tzu Hsi's last words, when she knew she was dying, were a warning never again to let a woman hold supreme power, and never to allow eunuchs to meddle in government affairs.

Unfortunately, she had not followed her own advice. Li Lien-ying built up such a nationwide system of graft and "squeeze" on official appointments that it brought him a fortune of at least ten million dollars. He encouraged the Empress' extravagances because so much of everything that was spent at court found its way into his own pockets. He also interfered in political matters. His hatred of Emperor Kuang Hsü played a part in the collapse of that ruler's early attempts at reform in 1898. His belief in the supposed supernatural powers of the Boxers, and his advice to the Empress to support them, was a major factor in her disastrous policy.

Until 1894, it was still just possible for the court to maintain the illusion of an all-powerful China. This illusion was shattered by a confrontation with Japan over Korea. The Yi Dynasty in Korea, having reigned for over five hundred years, was now in decline, and the country was split up into a number of opposing factions, unable to agree upon anything. In particular, they could not agree on how to meet the impact of Western culture. Korea had maintained her isolation longer than China or Japan, but by 1880, it was clear that she could no longer do so; the question was whether she should imitate Japan and accept Western technology whole-heartedly, or whether she should follow China and cling to the old, conservative, Confucian ways.

Throughout the Manchu Dynasty, Korea had acknowledged Chinese suzerainty and sent annual tribute missions to Peking. The Japanese had accepted this state of affairs reluctantly, never forgetting that Korea in the hands of an unfriendly power would be "a dagger pointing at the heart of Japan." Now, as Japan emerged from her isolation and moved into the modern world, she was determined to gain a foothold there.

By 1885, both China and Japan had troops stationed in Korea, and hostilities were only prevented when the two countries signed a treaty agreeing to withdraw these forces and to take no further action in Korea without consulting one another. Riots in Korea in 1894, however, led to both China and Japan sending in more troops without consultation. Japan then proposed that the two countries jointly take over the government of Korea, and China retorted that she would not interfere in the internal affairs of a vassal state such as Korea. Japan replied by seizing the royal palace at Seoul and sinking a Chinese ship which was carrying reinforcements to Korea. Five days later, on August 1, she declared war on China.

Most observers had no doubt of the outcome. China's armies were far larger, she had more ships, and there was every reason to think that her sheer size and weight of manpower would be overwhelming. Within the last thirty years, however, Japan had not only transformed her economy; she had mastered Western ideas of strategy and had trained and equipped a modern army and navy. It was superior skill and fire-power, not numbers, that counted now. With the outbreak of war, moreover, the country stood united, with all parties rallying to the support of the military.

The Sino-Japanese War

Chinese forces were quickly driven out of Korea into Manchuria. The Chinese fleet was defeated in a single battle near
the mouth of the Yalu River in September, 1894, and the ships
that survived this encounter took refuge first in Port Arthur
and then in Weihaiwei, where they were pursued by the Japanese and eventually forced to surrender. Port Arthur itself, a
naval base on the Liaotung Peninsula which had been strongly
fortified against attack by sea, was stormed from the rear and
taken in one bloody battle in November. The Japanese then
pushed on across Manchuria, almost within striking distance
of Peking. Many adventurous spirits must have remembered

*The Japanese attack on Weihaiwei during the
Sino-Japanese War, Japanese print of 1895.* COURTESY, THE
TRUSTEES OF THE BRITISH MUSEUM, LONDON

Hideyoshi's attempt to conquer China through Korea exactly three hundred years before and dreamed of succeeding where he had failed.

Defeat at the hands of these Dwarf Men, as the Chinese called them, was even more bitter than at the hands of the Western barbarians. China was, nevertheless, forced to sue for peace, and a treaty was concluded at Shimonoseki in April, 1895. Korea was to be independent of China, which meant that the Japanese were free to use as much influence and force there as they liked. The tip of the Liaotung Peninsula, with Dairen and Port Arthur (so named by the British in 1860, because a Lieutenant Arthur first discovered what an excellent harbor it was) was ceded to Japan. So were Taiwan and the Pescadores, giving Japan a string of islands which reached almost to the Chinese mainland. In addition to a large indemnity, China also agreed to grant Japan all the commercial privileges which Western nations now enjoyed in the Treaty Ports.

The effects of the war and the treaty of Shimonoseki were far-reaching, and disastrous for China. Japan had not merely defeated her great neighbor and dictated peace on her own terms. She had shown that she was now a military power to be reckoned with; and she had won a place among the Western nations who were now competing for concessions and territorial advantages in China.

Her astonishing military victory was soon followed by a diplomatic defeat. Russia, France and Germany, alarmed by this sudden shift in the balance of power in Asia, intervened to warn Japan that her occupation of the Liaotung Peninsula would violate the territorial integrity of China and advised her, in the interests of peace, to hand it back. Since it was obvious that Russia, at least, would fight if Japan did not follow this "advice," she reluctantly yielded to the so-called Triple Intervention.

If Japan had had any illusions about the nature of Russia's interest in Liaotung they were dispelled three years later when Russia forced the Chinese to grant her a twenty-five-year lease on that same Liaotung Peninsula, including Port Arthur. This gave Russia what she had always wanted: an ice-free Pacific port. (Ironically, a breakwater built by the Russians to deepen the harbor altered the flow of the warm ocean current, and the waters did freeze for the first time.) But Japan had learned that the only thing that mattered in this cynical struggle for national interests was superior military might. She did not forget. As soon as Russia had occupied Port Arthur, it became clear that the next clash in Korea and in Manchuria would be between Russia and Japan.

Meanwhile, China's weakness had been so cruelly revealed that other countries hastened to make the most of it. Germany obtained a ninety-nine-year lease of Tsingtao and its excellent harbor, with mining and railroad concessions in Shantung Province. France leased the Bay of Kwangchow, in Kwangtung Province, with permission to build railroads in the provinces adjoining Indochina. Russia, having already occupied all territory north of the Amur River, plus a coastal strip running south to the Korean border, now obtained permission to build a railway across northern Manchuria to connect with her Trans-Siberian Railroad. Britain, although she had refused to take part in the Triple Intervention, was worried by Russia's occupation of Port Arthur, and she insisted on leasing Weihaiwei, the port on the Gulf of Chihli immediately opposite the Liaotung Peninsula, for as long as Russia held the Manchurian port. She also acquired a long lease on mainland territory across the bay from Hongkong.

China was helpless to resist. For a time it looked as though the ancient Middle Kingdom, All under Heaven, might well be torn apart by the barbarians and cease to exist as a nation.

15. *The Hundred Days'*

Reform and the Boxer

Rebellion

WHEN HER SON Emperor T'ung Chih died in 1875, aged nineteen and without an heir, the Empress Dowager placed a four-year-old nephew of hers upon the throne with the reign title of Kuang Hsü. This was against all tradition. The boy was of the same generation as T'ung Chih, and therefore could not be adopted as his predecessor's son, nor perform the necessary ancestral sacrifices to the spirit of T'ung Chih. It also ignored the fact that T'ung Chih's Empress was expecting a child, who, if a boy, would be the rightful heir to the throne. Nothing, however, stood in Tzu Hsi's way once she had made up her mind. She now became Regent for the second time, whereas if a son of T'ung Chih's had come to the throne, his mother would have been Regent and Tzu Hsi would have been relegated to a minor position. T'ung Chih's Empress conveniently died before the child was born—officially a suicide— more likely a victim of her mother-in-law's ambitions.

Tzu Hsi retained full powers as Regent until 1889, when she handed over the government to Kuang Hsü. She then retired to her Summer Palace outside Peking, but she still kept in close touch with the Forbidden City, and everything that happened at court was immediately reported to her.

Kuang Hsü's education had been conservative and classical. He had little understanding of the modern world. He was, however, an intelligent, conscientious man, and it was as clear to him as it was to others of his generation that something must be done if the Manchu Dynasty, and indeed China itself, were to survive.

The Sino-Japanese War had revealed the extent of China's peril, but there was still no agreement on how best to meet it. Many Chinese leaders urged a continuation of the policy of Self-strengthening, borrowing Western techniques while preserving Chinese culture; others were convinced that they must follow Japan in a complete uprooting of the ancient ways; others simply hoped that the inevitable crisis would not come in their lifetime. Men like Sun Yat-sen were already openly— although from abroad—preaching the overthrow of the dynasty and the establishment of a republic. Emperor Kuang Hsü, however, hoped that he would be able to impose the much-needed reforms from above, through the monarchy and with a minimum of violence, as Emperor Meiji had done in Japan.

The Emperor was much influenced at this time by the ideas of a young Cantonese scholar, K'ang Yu-wei. K'ang Yu-wei, although a radical, was loyal to the monarchy. He believed that it would be possible to introduce sweeping changes without undermining the existing system. In the hundred days from June 11 to September 21, 1898, on the advice of K'ang Yu-wei and others of his reform party, the Emperor accordingly issued a series of Decrees on education, the armed forces, reforming the law, the police and the postal service, and on government

Empress Dowager Tzu Hsi, with Ladies in Waiting.
FROM A PHOTOGRAPH TAKEN IN 1903

administration. The civil service examinations were to be revised to include practical subjects, contemporary politics and the history of countries other than China. New schools were to teach Western learning as well as Chinese. Every attempt was to be made to stamp out corruption, beginning with the abolition of the many official positions which had become sinecures, unnecessary but very profitable to their holders.

208

The attack on these privileged positions, and the proposed changes in the examinations, caused dismay among the conservatives. The Empress Dowager was equally dismayed. Relations between the Old Buddha and Kuang Hsü had been outwardly friendly in the years since she retired, but the gulf between them had widened steadily, as he became more liberal, and she more reactionary. Opposing parties formed around them, nicknamed the Old Mother's Set and the Young Lad's Set. At first, the Empress and her party had been able to go along with the policy of Self-strengthening, but as the reformers' ideas became more radical they drew back even from that.

During the Hundred Days of Reform, conservatives flocked to the Summer Palace to beg the Empress to resume power, since only she could put an end to this dangerous nonsense. Tzu Hsi, by now completely out of sympathy with any proposed reforms, readily agreed to their plans for a coup d'etat which would remove Kuang Hsü from the throne once and for all.

Kuang Hsü and K'ang Yu-wei were warned of the proposed coup. Their only hope lay in striking first. They knew, however, that very few even among the Chinese officials, and probably no Manchu, would dare oppose the will of the Empress Dowager, and that if they were to succeed they must have the army behind them. In this dilemma, the Emperor called upon Yüan Shih-k'ai, a protégé of Li Hung-chang's who had played a leading part in the early stages of the Sino-Japanese War. Yüan's enemies claimed, perhaps with reason, that it was his over-confidence which had led China, unprepared as she was, into the war. His prestige at court, nevertheless, remained high, and Emperor Kuang Hsü trusted him, believing that Yüan was a true liberal who could bring the army over to their cause.

At their final meeting, Yüan Shih-k'ai, pledging his loyalty, received a small arrow as the symbol of his authority to carry out the Emperor's orders. These orders were to assassinate Jung Lu, the commander-in-chief of the northern armies, a man totally loyal to the Empress Dowager, and then quickly to surround the Summer Palace and take Tzu Hsi herself into custody before she could be warned of the danger. Having sworn obedience, Yüan Shih-k'ai immediately betrayed the plot to both Jung Lu and the Empress Dowager.

Within two hours, Tzu Hsi had summoned the Grand Council to a secret meeting at the Summer Palace, while troops loyal to her were sent to take over key points in the Forbidden City. Kuang Hsü was taken prisoner as he left the palace early the next morning, and then held captive on a small island in one of the lakes bordering on the Forbidden City. K'ang Yu-wei escaped and fled the country, but the other principal reformers were promptly executed, and the reform measures revoked.

Tzu Hsi, becoming Regent for the third time, now issued a Decree in the name of Kuang Hsü in which he lamented his own incompetence and recalled that during the Empress Dowager's former Regencies her exceptional abilities had enabled her to cope with every crisis.

"We have repeatedly besought Her Majesty to condescend once more to administer the government," the Decree continued; "Now she has graciously honored Us by granting Our prayer, a blessing indeed for all Our subjects. From this day forth Her Majesty will transact the business of government. . . ."

So ended the last hope of peaceful reform within the framework of the Manchu Dynasty. Chinese reformers, with the help of a Manchu Emperor, had sought to preserve the monarchy while modernizing the structure of government and education, to restore something of the glory of the past, and enable China to face other nations of the world as an equal. They had failed. Change must come, and now it could only come with the overthrow of the dynasty.

The opening of the twentieth century thus found China in desperate straits. Foreign pressure was mounting, and it seemed probable that the existing spheres of influence would become outright colonies. The Chinese navy had been destroyed, her army decisively defeated. The government had borrowed large sums of money to pay indemnities to Japan after the Sino-Japanese War, as well as to finance railroads, mines and other developments in China itself, so that Chinese resources were mortgaged to foreign governments. Yet every effort to halt corruption in the court and the central government had failed; even the most honest and patriotic statesmen were caught up in the network of bribery and corruption, with the eunuch Li Lien-ying and the Empress Dowager herself at its heart.

It is not surprising that the hated barbarians were held to blame for everything. If they had not forced their way into China, the argument ran, the Middle Kingdom could have continued to follow her ancient way of life indefinitely. Nor were the Chinese and their Manchu rulers necessarily mistaken in this; as long as she had not come into contact with the modern world, China's economy had been stable, and, at her own level of technology, she had made good use of her resources. It followed that if foreign influences were erased, China could return to the past.

The wiser statesmen and scholars, the students who had traveled abroad, the military men who had seen what Japan had done within a generation, knew that this was now impossible. China could no longer ignore the outside world in the hope that it would go away. But there were others less well informed and less clear thinking. Resentment against the foreigners, especially the missionaries, was widespread both in the government and among the people. The Secret Societies, the revolutionaries, all those who in previous centuries would have revolted against a corrupt and dying dynasty, were now diverted into antiforeign, anti-Christian movements.

The Society of Harmonious Fists, an offshoot of the ancient White Lotus Society, originated in Shantung Province before the turn of the century. Its slogan, echoing the Japanese "Revere the Emperor! Expel the foreigner!" was "Destroy the foreigner! Protect the Dynasty!" Its purpose was to drive out or murder all foreigners and all Christian converts, destroying Western influence wherever it was found. Men with foreign clothing or using foreign tools, were forced to burn these publicly; Christian converts, known as Secondary Devils, were liable to death.

The Boxers, as Westerners called the Harmonious Fists,

claimed that they were invulnerable to any weapon, including
the bullets of the hated foreigners. The Empress Dowager Tzu
Hsi seems to have believed this and secretly, if not openly,
encouraged their anti-foreign activities.

Many missionaries who were forced to flee from provinces
where the Boxer movement was strong took refuge in Peking.
There, in the summer of 1900, thousands of foreigners, diplomats, missionaries, businessmen, and Chinese Christians, found
themselves trapped by the Boxers, who threatened to massacre
the entire community. The Peking government, either genuinely, or pretending to be concerned for their safety, ordered
all foreigners to leave the city immediately, offering them safe
conduct and an armed escort to the coast. Although this meant
abandoning the native Christians to almost certain death and
torture, and although they knew that it might well be a trap
to deliver them into the hands of the Boxers, their situation was
so desperate that they agreed to go. Meanwhile, however, the
German Minister was murdered in the streets of Peking while
on his way to negotiate with the Foreign Office. This convinced the foreigners that the Manchu Government could not,
even if it wanted to, guarantee their safety outside their own
Legations; their only hope would be to hold out there until help
came from abroad.

It was a forlorn hope. Most of the foreigners, with a few
hundred of their own troops, were besieged in what was called
the Legation Quarter, where eleven Legations were loosely
grouped together, surrounded by Chinese houses and shops, and
overlooked by the city wall. Several thousand others, mostly

Chinese Christians, were cut off in Peitang, a Catholic cathedral in the northwest of the city. Food and water soon ran short at Peitang, and many of the refugees were near starvation before relief came; the Legations were better off because there were two wells inside the Quarter, and a stable of riding horses provided fresh meat.

The Boxers alone might not have been a serious threat if the government had disavowed them. But on June 21, the Empress Dowager declared war against the foreign powers, and imperial troops were ordered to join in the assault on the Legations. Cheered by the (mistaken) belief that a relief column of foreign troops was almost at the city gates, the beleaguered foreigners fought back with everything they had; non-combatants piled up sandbags, strengthened the walls of the Legations with makeshift barricades and organized fire-fighting and hospital units.

Fire was the greatest danger. On June 23, the wind being from the north, fanatical Chinese soldiers set fire to the Hanlin Academy, just north of the British Legation, in the hope that the fire would spread to the Legations. The wind veered suddenly, and the Legations were saved, but the beautiful buildings of the Hanlin were burnt to the ground, and its many treasures, including the only complete copy of Yung Lo's great Encyclopedia of the fifteenth century, were lost.

In the weeks that followed, casualties were heavy, and it seemed almost impossible that the Legations and Peitang could hold out from one day to the next. Yet there was a strange ambivalence about the fighting. The Empress Dowager undoubtedly meant to drive out or massacre all foreign nationals, and in spite of their brave defense the Legations and Peitang could have been overrun at any time by a full-scale attack. Such an attack never came. Clearly, someone in authority had realized that still further calamities would befall China if the foreigners were massacred, and was determined to save their lives. In fact, it seems to have been Jung Lu himself, commander-in-chief of the imperial northern armies, who, having failed to persuade Tzu Hsi to moderate her policy, now staged a noisy attack on the Legations, taking care never to push it too far. When the position was most desperate, in July, a twelve-day truce was called so that fresh supplies could be sent in to the besieged foreigners.

Jung Lu was not alone in his wisdom. Chinese viceroys in the south and in Shantung, refused to recognize Peking's declaration of war. They informed the foreign powers that they would remain neutral and would outlaw the Boxers in their own provinces, protecting foreign lives, as long as the foreigners took no military action against them. The war was thus confined to the north, around Peking, Tientsin and in the neighboring province of Shansi.

In June, the Empress Dowager had sent out a secret Decree to provincial governers, ordering them to kill every foreigner in their area; even if the foreigners were willing to leave the country, they should not be allowed to do so, but must be executed. Before this Decree was actually sent, however, two of the Empress' senior advisers managed to alter the word "kill" to the word "protect." Their deception came to light when the governor of Shansi, who was bitterly anti-foreign, sent back a memorial asking whether the Empress really meant that he must protect the foreigners. Tzu Hsi replied with a second Decree ordering all foreigners, young and old, men, women and children, to be put to death: "Let not one escape, so that my empire may be purged of this noisome source of corruption, and that peace may be restored to my loyal subjects."

The governor of Shansi enthusiastically carried out this order, personally presiding over the execution of forty-six missionaries. The Empress soon discovered the identity of the two men who had tampered with the original decree. They were decapitated, but their brave action had, meanwhile, saved the lives of many other foreigners.

The Old Buddha herself was beginning to have doubts about the wisdom of her policy. During the July truce, she had shown a surprising change of heart by sending gifts of watermelons, vegetables and wine to the foreigners and inquiring anxiously about their health. By August, she must have realized that the invulnerable Boxers could be killed as easily as other men. By August, also, an expeditionary force made up of the soldiers of eight nations, with some Chinese recruits, had taken the Taku Forts and the city of Tientsin and was moving towards Peking.

The relief force might have moved faster had it not been for disputes among the countries involved, as well as the difficulties of mounting an international invasion of so distant and so alien a country. The token forces provided by Germany, Austria and Italy soon retired, while the French were too few in number to play an active part. The march on Peking was led by the Japanese, Russians, British and Americans; the Japanese were not only the largest contingent, but their behavior in such difficult circumstances was apparently the most admirable.

British troops entered the city on August 14, when they broke through a small gate in the south wall of the city and, closely followed by their allies, reached the Legation Quarter without opposition. Peitang, the Cathedral in the north city which had been in even greater peril than the Legations, was relieved a day later.

The Empress Dowager fled from Peking the very night that the allies entered the city, insisting that Emperor Kuang Hsü accompany her. No preparations had been made for the flight, and the scene must have been chaotic as the Old Buddha, wearing the blue cloth clothes of a Chinese peasant, her hair pulled back Chinese style, her long fingernails cut short, made ready for the journey. At the last moment, Kuang Hsü's beloved Pearl Concubine rashly begged the Empress Dowager to allow the Emperor to stay behind, so that he might be with his people in their time of trouble. Tzu Hsi, who already hated the Pearl Concubine because of her loyalty to Kuang Hsü after the coup d'etat of 1898, thereupon ordered her attendants to drop the unfortunate girl down a nearby well and throw stones on top of her. The grief-stricken Emperor, the Empress Dowager and her bedraggled party then set out on what was officially described as an Autumn Tour of Inspection in the Western Provinces.

It could truthfully be called a tour. Two months and seven hundred miles later, the party, swollen as other fleeing officials caught up with them, reached Sian, ancient Ch'ang-an. There, Tzu Hsi set up a court in exile, leaving the faithful but now elderly Li-Hung-chang in Peking to negotiate peace terms with the victorious allies. Peking, which had already suffered so much from the fighting and had been plundered by the Boxers, was looted again by the foreigners—military and civilian alike. An incredible amount of treasure, works of art, curios and even the astronomical instruments in the Observatory were carried away, although the astronomical instruments, at least, were later returned.

The Boxer Protocol was signed in September, 1901, more than a year after the entry of foreign troops into Peking. It provided for a huge indemnity (over three hundred and thirty million dollars, with interest to be added); for the Legation Quarter to be enlarged, walled and fortified; for the execution of the most violently anti-foreign leaders, including the governor of Shansi; formal apologies, the suppression of anti-foreign Societies, and other conditions designed to secure the safety of foreigners in China.

Had it not been for the level-headed provincial governors outside Peking, and for Li Hung-chang's skill in persuading the Powers to accept the fiction that there had been no war—only a rebellion—China might well have been partitioned among the foreign Powers at this time. She was no longer sovereign within her own borders. Russia had occupied Manchuria. Other Western countries stationed large forces in Peking and north China, while foreign warships patrolled Chinese coastal waters and the Yangtze River.

And the Old Buddha, whose stubbornness had played a major part in this debacle? She now declared that she had never favored the Boxers; anyone who believed that the government had supported their anti-foreign movement must have overlooked her many Decrees calling for the Christians to be protected and the Boxers to be suppressed. To make this quite clear she ordered all Decrees issued between June 20 and August 14 to be submitted to her, so that "spurious or illegal documents may be withdrawn and canceled." Having thus rewritten history, she returned in triumph to Peking in January, 1902, warmly welcomed by Manchu, Chinese and foreigner alike. A few weeks later she received the representatives of the foreign Powers, and then their wives; the latter presented an address expressing their pleasure at the return of Her Majesty to her capital, and were much impressed by her friendliness and charm.

Meanwhile, Tzu Hsi had come to the conclusion that the government, the armed forces and the educational system of the country must be completely reorganized. An edict issued in 1901, while skillfully praising the virtues and ideals of the reactionary party and the rigid Confucianists, went far toward adopting the very measures which K'ang Yu-wei and the unfortunate Kuang Hsü had proposed in 1898. It seemed possible that this remarkable woman, using her surprising new popularity among the people, might succeed in pushing through the reforms which she herself had defeated only a few years before.

There was, however, very little time left for peaceful reform. One crisis followed another, and now Russia and Japan were moving toward a new war which would be fought on the borders of China and in Chinese waters and in which China, although helpless to take part, would be deeply concerned.

16. The Russo-

Japanese War

CENTURY BY CENTURY, Russia had been pushing further across the wastes of northern Asia. She had reached the shores of the Pacific Ocean and moved across the narrow Bering Straits into what is now Alaska, although she later sold her rights there to the United States. Her territories in Asia and Europe were vast, but for a long time they did not include an ice-free port in either hemisphere which could be used as a naval base the year round. In the west, the Dardanelles were closed to foreign warships, so that the Russian navy had no outlet from the Black Sea, and the Baltic was by no means ice-free; in the Pacific, Vladivostok was far north and was frozen throughout the winter.

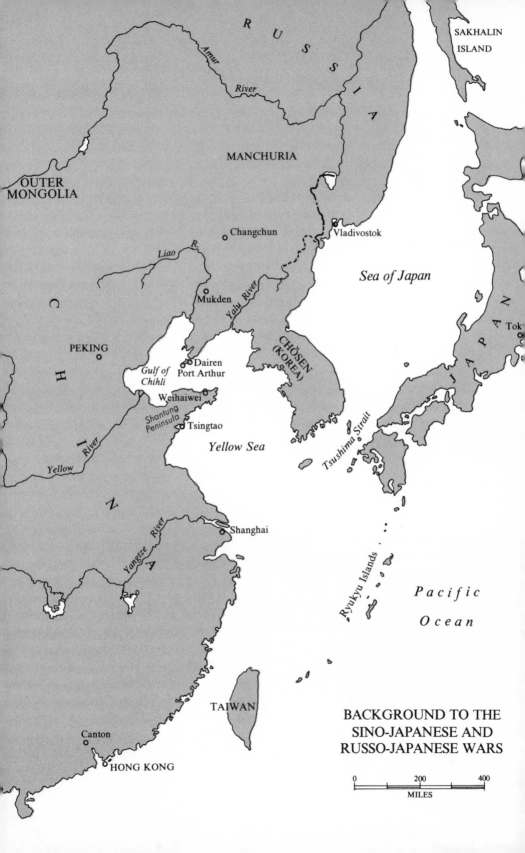

R U S S I A

SAKHALIN
ISLAND

Amur

MANCHURIA

River

OUTER
MONGOLIA

Changchun

Vladivostok

Sea of Japan

Liao *R.*

Mukden

Yalu River

CHŌSEN
(KOREA)

J
A
P
A
N

Tok

PEKING

Dairen
Port Arthur

Gulf of
Chihli

C
H
I

Weihaiwei

Shantung
Peninsula

Tsingtao

Yellow Sea

Tsushima Strait

N
A

River

Yellow

Z

Yangtze River

Shanghai

Ryukyu Islands

Pacific

Ocean

TAIWAN

Canton

BACKGROUND TO THE
SINO-JAPANESE AND
RUSSO-JAPANESE WARS

HONG KONG

0   200   400

MILES

Russia's determination to obtain such a port was at last fulfilled in 1898, when she "persuaded" China to grant her a lease on the Liaotung Peninsula, with its excellent harbor, Port Arthur. This became the main base for her Pacific fleet. The Boxer uprisings in 1900 provided her with an excuse to occupy the hinterland as well, and although she claimed that this was a temporary measure to assure the safety of her nationals and her communications, she showed no sign of withdrawing once the crisis was past.

Other foreign powers felt that their interests in Manchuria, north China and East Asia as a whole, were threatened by the Russian encroachment. It also violated the Open Door policy which had first been expounded by the United States in 1899, and somewhat reluctantly accepted by the other powers. Although the doctrine of the Open Door was not as altruistic as it sounds, since its object was to keep the door open to economic penetration by all countries equally (an up-to-date version of the "most-favored-nation" clause in the unequal treaties), it did help prevent the break-up of China into colonies where one power could have excluded all the others. Now that Russia held Port Arthur, however, she was not inclined to listen to any argument that the other powers should have equal rights in Manchuria.

Japan was especially vulnerable. Once Russia was established in Manchuria, there was little doubt that she would seek to occupy, or at least dominate, the Korean Peninsula which jutted out between her two major ports, Vladivostok on the north Pacific, and Port Arthur on the Gulf of Chihli. Japan would then be faced by a great power in control of mainland territory which was almost on her doorstep, a power with a strong, modern fleet and with direct railroad links to factories and dockyards in Europe. This was a danger greater even than the ancient but unforgotten menace of the Mongol empire under Kublai Khan. In such a situation, moreover, Japan would have lost all hope of establishing herself on the mainland of Asia.

When it became clear that the Russians did not intend to

withdraw more than a few token troops from the forces they had stationed in Manchuria, Japan tried to negotiate. Talks dragged on. Russia steadfastly refused to give any guarantee that she would recognize Japan's special position in Korea, even if Japan agreed to recognize her special position in Manchuria. Meanwhile, in 1902, Japan signed an alliance with Britain, who was also much concerned about Russia's advances in Asia. This Anglo-Japanese Alliance did not bind either party to come to the aid of the other against a single power, but only if a second country were to join in the fight against them; it did mean that in the event of war between Russia and Japan, no other country could ally itself with Russia without running the risk of war with England.

It had become clear to Japan, both from the Triple Intervention and from her own experiences during the Allied Expeditionary Force sent to relieve the Legations in Peking, that influence in the modern world was measured by the military strength behind it. During her early contacts with the West, trade, firearms and Christianity had seemed to go together, and some converts to Christianity thought that the secret of the foreigners' strength lay in their religion. By the end of the nineteenth century, however, the Japanese had realized that there was a great gap between the words and the deeds of the foreign Christians; that their merchants were as greedy, their military men as quarrelsome and their politicians as unscrupulous as any non-Christian. It was their cannon and their gunboats that counted. This led to the increasing influence of the military party in Japan, and its insistence that more and more of the country's resources and manpower should be devoted to building an army and navy equal to that of any European power. (At the same time, the number of Christian converts declined noticeably.)

Few people outside Japan believed that she would go to war with the giant, Russia. Geography was in Japan's favor to the extent that Russia's bases in Manchuria were at the end of the long, single-track Trans-Siberian Railway, and any ships not already stationed in the Far East would have to travel all the way from the Baltic Sea, whereas Japan would be operating in home waters. Men and supplies could be quickly replaced, repairs carried out immediately. Such advantages, however, were balanced by the fact that Japan would be risking everything, with her own country open to invasion if she failed, while a Russian defeat in the Pacific would not threaten the European heart of her empire.

Japan broke off negotiations early in February, 1904. Two days later, without any formal declaration of war, Japanese ships made a surprise attack on the Russian fleet off Port Arthur and sank or disabled several Russian warships. The Russians were so disorganized by this unexpected setback that the remainder of their fleet did not dare put to sea for some time. Japan, meanwhile, gained control of the China Sea and the Straits of Korea, and was able to ferry her armies across to the Korean Peninsula without interference. In the months that followed, these troops advanced north and west, winning one victory after another over the Russians and gradually pushing across Manchuria until they finally took the capital city, Mukden, in 1905.

Other Japanese armies, meanwhile, besieged and captured Port Arthur. Unable to approach the fortress by sea because of its great guns, they had attacked on the landward side, which proved almost equally impregnable. It was only after five months of bitter fighting and heavy casualties, against a heroic defense, that the city and its magnificent harbor at last fell to them in January, 1905.

Despite these successes on land, the final outcome could only be decided at sea. If the Russian navy defeated the Japanese and won control of the China seas, cutting the Japanese lines of communication, then the Japanese forces on the mainland would be not only useless—they would be wiped out. And there was no doubt that the Russian Baltic Fleet, which had already put to sea in October, 1904 on the first leg of a long journey to the Pacific, was far stronger on paper than anything the Japanese could muster. They were handicapped, however, by having to sail all the way around Africa, since

The Battle of Tsushima,
contemporary Japanese print.

Britain would not allow them to use the Suez Canal, and by the problem of refueling. Coal, which was the fuel used in those days, was much more difficult to handle than oil is now, and neutral ports everywhere were closed to the warships of a belligerent nation. Their speed was also reduced because they had no opportunity to scrape their hulls.

The morale of the Russian sailors was low. Many of the

officers and men had come from the land, trained to work a ship's engines or its guns, but with little feeling for the vessel as a whole, and little if any practice in joint maneuvers. The increasing political ferment in Russia, where revolution was already brewing, was reflected in discontent and insubordination among the ships' crews. At Madagascar, where they heard the shattering news of the Japanese conquest of Port Arthur,

the fleet was delayed for over two months by illness and mutiny. Under command of a less determined admiral, they might well have turned back.

Admiral Rodjestvenski, on the contrary, well aware that the outcome of the war now depended entirely on him and his ships, pressed on across the Indian Ocean and into the Pacific, as fast as the fleet could steam. Now that Port Arthur was lost to them, Vladivostok was the only harbor where the Russian ships could be repaired, refueled and their crews rested, and the Admiral was hoping to reach there before encountering the Japanese navy. He, therefore, took the most direct route to the north, through the dangerously narrow Straits of Tsushima. And there, Admiral Togo, already victorious in several naval battles against the Russian ships which had been based at Port Arthur, was waiting for him.

The encounter which followed is generally described as the greatest sea battle since Trafalgar. Its outcome was one of the most unexpected and most dramatic in all naval history. Admiral Togo brought his ships across the line of the Russian advance in the classic maneuver known as "Crossing the T," firing broadsides with deadly effect as the enemy ships, one by one, came within range. The Russian fleet was forced to swing east and then south, heading away from their haven at Vladivostok, with the Japanese in pursuit. The battle raged throughout the day, and Japanese torpedo boats, against which the Russian ships were helpless, carried on the fight by night. Next morning, what was left of the Russian fleet, with the exception of a few small vessels which found refuge in neutral harbors such as Manila, either surrendered or were sunk by their own men. One ship, when all hope was gone, ran a white tablecloth up the mast for want of anything else.

It was a staggering disaster. Thirty-two out of the thirty-five Russian warships were destroyed or disabled, and an estimated two-thirds of their men were lost. The superiority of Japanese seamanship, the training and professional pride of her sailors, and the condition of her ships, few in number but recently overhauled and refitted in her home ports, had proved more than equal to the apparently mighty but disorganized and travel-weary Russian fleet.

The impact of the victory was enormous. For the first time, an Asiatic power had decisively defeated a Western power in a full-scale war on both land and sea. On the other side of

the world, news of the annihilation of their fleet led to out-
breaks of violence in St. Petersburg. In Asia, Japan was in a
position to dictate terms to her enemy. The Japanese, however,
had thrown their heart and their treasure into the struggle, and
they were exhausted by it; they had neither the men nor the
resources to follow up their success by occupying Manchuria,
and they, therefore, asked President Roosevelt to take the
initiative in negotiating a peace treaty. The United States was
more than willing to do so, for although they had regarded the
Russian advance into Manchuria and north China with alarm,
they certainly had no wish to see Japan all-powerful there.

The Treaty, signed in Portsmouth, New Hampshire, in Sep-
temper, 1905, restored Chinese sovereignty—for what it was
worth—in Manchuria and transferred the Russian lease on the
Liaotung Peninsula to Japan. It gave Japan the Russian-built
South Manchurian Railway running from Liaotung through
Mukden and north to Changchun, as well as the southern half
of Sakhalin Island, north of the Japanese archipelago. Russia
also recognized Japan's special position in Korea. Since China
was now too weak to exercise any influence over Korea, this
meant that Japan had a free hand there, and within a few
months Korea had been declared a Japanese protectorate, with
a Resident General as Governor, and all idea of true independence had been lost. This was followed by outright annexa-
tion in 1910.

From 1910, until Korea at last regained her independence
in 1945, Japan did everything possible to absorb her unfortunate neighbor, culturally, educationally and militarily. The
Korean army was disbanded. The Japanese, either directly or
through "advisers," controlled Korean administration, industry,
finance, police, schools and other institutions. It was forbidden
to teach Korean history or the Korean language, Japanese being
used exclusively. Thousands of lower class Japanese immigrated
to Korea to take advantage of their now privileged position
there, and Korean workers suffered accordingly. It is a tribute
to the character of the Korean people that they nevertheless
preserved their own culture, and were never truly assimilated.

The Meiji era in Japan came to an end in 1912 with the death of Emperor Meiji. His lifetime had seen the country transformed. Japan was now a modern industrial nation and an imperial power. She was just as interested in expansion and in carving out spheres of influence in weaker countries as any Western power, and equally able to do so. Her soldiers were soon to acquire a reputation for aggressiveness, even brutality, in contrast to the high standard of discipline and chivalry towards the defeated, which they had shown before and during the Russo-Japanese War. (Admittedly, this often depended, as in any country, on individual leaders. In the Russo-Japanese War, both Admiral Togo and General Nogi, who commanded at the siege of Port Arthur, were men of outstanding ability, character and honor.)

Far more important than the impact of the war on the Western powers, who now had to admit the presence of an Asian nation among them, was the effect on nationalist movements throughout Asia. There were already revolutionary nationalist parties in China, India, the Dutch East Indies and the Philippines, with men who dreamed of being strong enough to drive out the foreigners and restore sovereignty to their own people. In the late nineteenth century, at the peak of Western imperialism, this had seemed a dream or, at best, a hope in the distant future. Now, with the example of Japan, it became a possibility worth fighting for in the present. From the time of the Russo-Japanese War, independence movements throughout Asia took heart, and the tide turned slowly in their favor.

17. *The Revolution*

of 1911

IN THE HOUR of Japan's triumph over Russia, China remained
as helpless as ever, caught in the same vicious spiral of
government corruption and foreign exploitation. The Empress
Dowager Tzu Hsi, the formidable Old Buddha, who was now
over seventy, still held absolute power as Regent. Kuang Hsü,
Emperor in name, lived on as a prisoner in his lakeside pavilion.
There was some surprise that he had survived, since Tzu Hsi
would probably have preferred to have him out of the way in
order to place another minor on the throne. Her failure to
have done so may have been caused by the fact that she knew
the Emperor's death would have been viewed with suspicion
among the foreigners, with whom she now kept on good terms;

or she may have been influenced by a strange rumor current in Peking to the effect that she herself would not outlive Kuang Hsü.

In fact, Kuang Hsü died on November 14, and the Empress on November 15, 1908. The strange coincidence of their deaths may have been simply coincidence, but it is also possible that the reactionary party, remembering the Hundred Days of Reform, made sure that Kuang Hsü should not survive her and return to power.

Some weeks earlier, the Old Buddha had chosen the infant Pu Yi, whose reign name was to be Hsüan T'ung, as Heir Apparent to Kuang Hsü. The boy's father, Prince Ch'un, who was Kuang Hsü's younger brother, was to become Regent, although the indefatigable Tzu Hsi apparently looked forward to sharing in yet another Regency in which she would have the upper hand.

Little time now remained to the Manchu Dynasty. Prince Ch'un could have been a greater man than he was, and yet been unable to hold back the storm which was about to break over China. One of his first actions, interesting in the light of past and future events, was to dismiss Yüan Shih-k'ai from court. Neither Emperor Kuang Hsü nor the new Regent had ever forgiven Yüan for his part in betraying the 1898 reformers to the Empress Dowager; even on his deathbed Kuang Hsü had dictated one last message, calling for Yüan Shih-k'ai's death: "When the times comes I desire that Yüan be summarily beheaded." Yüan, however, was so popular and had such influence over the northern armies that the new Regent did not dare follow this advice, and had to be content with exiling him from the court. Yüan Shih-k'ai's prestige with the army was to play a major part in the course of the coming Revolution.

Meanwhile the revolutionary movement was active both underground in China and abroad, where it was now led by Sun Yat-sen. Sun was a native of Kwangtung Province, as were many of the other revolutionaries, the southern Chinese being by nature more excitable, more politically-minded, more subject to violent upheavals than those of the north, and also more exposed to outside influences. Yet his career was far different from those of the rebels who had overthrown previous dynasties. He was not a military leader. He was a Christian, but of conventional faith, with none of the wild ideas of the leader of the Taipings; nor does he ever seem to have thought that the Mandate of Heaven might fall upon him personally.

Sun Yat-sen was representative of the new "Overseas Chinese," educated abroad, familiar with Western thought and convinced that reforms in China must be brought about by a complete overhaul of the system of government. There were many shades of opinion among the overseas students, but the majority, especially after the failure of the Hundred Days of Reform, were convinced that this could only be done by the abolition of the dynasty and the establishment of a Republic.

Sun Yat-sen was partly educated in Hawaii, where his older brother was living, and it was there that he first studied at a Christian school. Although he was not baptized until some years later, he seems to have been genuinely and lastingly converted to Christianity. It may also have seemed to him, as to other Christian converts, that the new society they envisioned for China would be best served by a new religion.

Returning home, Sun Yat-sen continued his education in Canton and in Hongkong, where he received a medical diploma. He even practiced medicine for a time in Macao, but his heart was already set on the revolution, and he was soon deeply involved in conspiracies to overthrow the existing order in China. In 1895, members of the Revive China Society, which he founded, tried to seize government headquarters in Canton, an attempt which failed miserably; fifteen of the sixteen conspirators were caught and executed, and Sun Yat-sen alone escaped.

Exiled, with a price on his head, Sun now traveled, talked, raised money among the overseas Chinese and openly preached the coming Revolution. He was not a great intellectual, nor a scholar in the classical sense, but he was well informed and widely read on political and economic theories, and his ideas were taking definite shape. He came increasingly to the conclusion that it was impossible to make changes gradually in the existing system, as K'ang Yu-wei and others after him had proposed. Instead, much impressed by Japan, he believed that China, under a revolutionary government, should break with the past and make one all-out effort which would speedily transform the country into a modern, well-governed, economically prosperous nation.

In Japan, in 1905, the Revive China Society and several other revolutionary groups were brought together with the founding of the T'ung Meng Hui, or United League (literally, Together Sworn Society or Society of those Sworn Together) with Sun Yat-sen as Chief Executive. The League stood for the overthrow and complete expulsion of the Manchus, establishment of a republican government, nationalization of the land, and world peace.

Sun Yat-sen and other members of the League were in touch with a network of conspirators and secret societies in China itself, especially in the south, the west and the Yangtze Valley, all working towards the same ends. There were several abortive attempts to take action, frustrated either by lack of coordination among the plotters, or because the government was forewarned. In 1910, an attempt to assassinate the Manchu Regent in Peking failed. In April, 1911, a further plot to seize government headquarters in Canton was also thwarted, with considerable loss of life.

The long overdue Revolution, which was finally to succeed and to destroy imperial China, broke out in October, 1911, almost by accident. Plans for an uprising in Hankow were discovered when a bomb exploded prematurely in the warehouse of the revolutionaries, and the conspirators had to act to save themselves. Soldiers in nearby Wuchang who were involved in the plot, mutinied and marched on the residence of the Manchu Viceroy, where they met with almost no resistance; the Viceroy and his commanding officers fled, and the People's Army, as they now called themselves, took over the city. Since there was no political figure or leader of the United League on hand to organize a new government, the rebel troops forced

THE EIGHTEEN PROVINCES
OF CHINA PROPER
(MODERN)

300 MILES

MANCHURIA

INNER MONGOLIA

Yellow River

KANSU

Peking

HOPEI

SHANSI

SHENSI

Wei R.

Yellow River

SHANTUNG

Yellow Sea

HONAN

KIANGSU

Nanking

Shanghai

ANHWEI

SZECHWAN

HUPEI

CHEKIANG

Yangtze River

KWEICHOU

HUNAN

KIANGSI

FUKIEN

YUNNAN

KWANGSI

KWANTUNG

Canton

TAIWAN

HONG KONG

BURMA

South China Sea

HAINAN

LAOS

VIETNAM

THAILAND

U.S.S.R.

JAPAN

CHINA

INDIA

their somewhat reluctant brigade commander to become the
leader of their unexpectedly successful rebellion.

This was the spark that set the country ablaze. The date was
October 10, the Double Tenth, or tenth day of the tenth month,
which later became the national day of the Chinese Republic.
There was no turning back now, and within the next few
days the whole of the sister cities of Hankow, Wuchang and
Hanyang (sometimes collectively known as Wuhan) had fallen
to the People's Army. Meanwhile Sun Yat-sen, who was in the
United States raising money for the campaign, learned from
the American papers that his Revolution had begun.

The Revolution quickly swept southern China. Shanghai
and other large cities rallied to its support. Some areas declared
themselves neutral, as did the representatives of the foreign
powers, but very few actively supported the Manchu regime.
Manchu garrisons and communities either fled as best they
could, or were slaughtered, men, women and children; there
was little resistance, for the Manchu Bannermen were ill
equipped and ill prepared, weakened by the general atmosphere
of fatalism and despair which had infected the government.

In this crisis, the Manchu Regent turned to Yüan Shih-k'ai,
whom he had dismissed from office three years earlier. There
was no one else. Yüan Shih-k'ai could command the loyalty of
the northern army, a disciplined and comparatively well-armed
fighting force which he had helped train, and which might yet
be able to put down the rebellion before it spread further.
Yüan took his time, delaying until he saw how the fighting
went and until he was sure he could dictate his own terms,
thereby throwing away the last hope, if there still was such a
hope, of saving the Dynasty. In November, despite the grim
picture, he agreed to become Prime Minister and commander-
in-chief, with full powers.

Moving his armies south, Yüan Shih-k'ai recaptured Hankow
and Hanyang, but he did not cross the river into Wuchang. He
had shown his strength. It is doubtful whether he ever intended
to do more than that; it seems likely that his objective, now, was
not to save the existing Dynasty but to force the Manchus

to abdicate, leaving himself in power to form a new government and possibly a new dynasty. In December, by which time the People's Army had captured Nanking, he agreed to negotiate a general settlement with the Revolutionary Party according to which the Manchus would abdicate, and a Republican Government would be set up in their place.

Sun Yat-sen, meanwhile, arrived in Shanghai, where he was proclaimed provisional President of the new Republic. He entered Nanking on January 1, 1912, to a salute of twenty-one guns, and there took the oath of allegiance. He swore then that once the Manchu Government had been deposed and peace had been restored to the country, he would establish a demo-

cratic government, based on the will of the people. This done, he would resign and the people themselvs would elect the first President of China.

The Provisional Government adopted the western solar calendar to replace the Chinese lunar calendar, and a new flag. The five equal stripes of the flag, yellow, red, blue, white and black, represented the five peoples, Chinese, Manchu, Mongol, Tibetan and Moslem, who were to be united in the Chinese Republic.

On January 5, the new government issued a manifesto addressed to all friendly nations announcing the establishment of the Chinese Republic, the outcome of a long fight for freedom. The Republican Government, it announced, would reform the civil and criminal codes, abolish restrictions on trade, reform the finances of the country and work for better relations with the rest of the world. They would honor all treaties, loans and concessions agreed to by the Manchu Government before the Revolution, and protect all foreigners. The manifesto, incidentally, blamed the Manchus for having shut the Middle Kingdom off from the western world. It recalled the Nestorian Tablet of 781 A.D. and the writings of Marco Polo as evidence of the former Chinese tolerance of foreigners and their religion, quite overlooking the fact that it was the native Ming Dynasty which had first isolated China from the outside world.

The last Manchu Emperor, Hsüan T'ung, or Pu Yi, now aged six, formally abdicated on February 12. He was allowed to maintain his imperial title and his residence in the Forbidden City, and he was granted a pension; the tombs of his ancestors were also to be maintained, with appropriate sacrifices made to their spirits. (In later years Pu Yi was driven from the For-

Officials fleeing from Tientsin during the Revolution of 1911.
RADIO TIMES HULTON PICTURE LIBRARY, LONDON

bidden City; still later, the Japanese installed him as Emperor of their puppet state of Manchukuo; he was captured by the Russians in 1945 and was eventually sent back to Communist China, where he was converted to Communism and worked as a gardener and librarian until the end of his life.) Thus the curtain fell on two and a half centuries of the great Ch'ing Dynasty. Now that the strong hand of the Empress Dowager was gone, Manchu resistance had been feeble. It was almost as though they realized that the natural span of the Dynasty had run its course. They had come in with the roar of a tiger, it was said, and now they slid from sight like the tail of a snake.

What was strange was not the downfall of the Manchus but the abruptness with which the very idea of imperial rule was discarded. Since Ch'in Shih Huang Ti in the third century B.C., a united Middle Kingdom ruled by an all-powerful Son of Heaven had been the only accepted form of government. The Emperor was the Pole Star around which the people, the administration, the world, revolved. Even in times of anarchy and civil war, the principle of imperial rule was not in question; rivals for the throne fought to see who held the Mandate of Heaven, and who, therefore, had both the right and the duty to rule All under Heaven. Now that there was to be a constitution and a parliament, with no single ruler, where did the Mandate of Heaven lie?

In theory, the Mandate was to be replaced by the will of the people. As early as 1905, when the United League was founded, Sun Yat-sen had stated the Three Principles of the People (San Min Chu-i) which should govern Republican China. These were Democracy, the government of the people,

for the people; Nationalism, the right to be free from foreign control; and Socialism, the right of all people to a sufficient livelihood. These broad principles were flexible enough to attract wide support, and they could be adapted to changing situations as freely as the now-discredited doctrines of Confucius had been. Revised and reinterpreted over the years, they were to remain the accepted basis of the Chinese Republic.

The will of the people, however, was almost bound to reflect the will of whoever held the most power at any given

time. Sun Yat-sen might be recognized as the main architect of the Revolution, and there was no doubt that he was now a figure of international repute, but it was Yüan Shih-k'ai who was most powerful within China. Yüan was the only man with influence in both imperial and republican circles; he had the strongest army, and only he had a reasonable chance of being able to maintain order in the country after the downfall of the monarchy. It was largely on his advice that the Manchus had abdicated, and the terms had been his, not those of Sun Yat-sen. Sun Yat-sen, therefore, resigned as Provisional President, as he had promised to do, and on his advice the National Council in Nanking elected Yüan Shih-k'ai, instead of himself, to be the first President of China. (Four years later Yüan tried to betray the Republic, as he had betrayed the Manchus, by proclaiming himself Emperor of a new dynasty, but in this he failed.)

The foreign powers generally remained neutral in the face of the Revolution. They could scarcely disapprove of Sun Yat-sen's Three Principles of the People, nor of his Christian ideals. Concerned to safeguard their investments and their trade, they were reassured by his promise that foreign treaties and concessions would be honored by the Republican Government. They were impressed by the character of Yüan Shih-k'ai, apparently a strong man, a leader willing and able to take the place of the discredited Manchu regime.

Even the most optimistic observers, Chinese and foreign, realized the magnitude of the problems facing the new Republic. But in the early months of 1912, it seemed as though a start had been made, and as though China were really moving toward the position in the world to which her size, her resources and the great qualities of her people entitled her. For a little time, the future looked bright.

Yüan Shih-k'ai, first President of China.
RADIO TIMES HULTON PICTURE LIBRARY, LONDON

CHRONOLOGICAL TABLE

	CHINA	NORTHERN TRIBES	JAPAN	KOREA
B.C.				
Before 1523	Mythical or legendary rulers			
ca.1523	Shang-Yin Dynasty			
ca.1027	Chou Dynasty	Hsiung-nu (Huns)	Prehistoric Cultures	Chinese Colonies founded 108 B.C.
255	Ch'in Dynasty			
206	Han Dynasty			
A.D.				
220-589	Division into several northern and southern Kingdoms	Various powerful nomad tribes including	Nara Culture 710-784	Before 668: The Three Kingdoms of:
589	Sui Dynasty			Koguryo Paekche
618	T'ang Dynasty	Khitan (Liao Dynasty)	Heian Culture 794-1185	Silla
960	Sung Dynasty	Juchen (Chin Dynasty)		Kingdom of Silla: 668-935
1279	Yüan Dynasty (Mongols)	Mongols (Genghiz Khan, died 1227)	Kamakura Shogunate 1185-1336	

	CHINA	NORTHERN TRIBES	JAPAN	KOREA
1368	Ming Dynasty	(Kublai Khan, died 1294)	(Mongol invasions: 1274 and 1281)	Kingdom of Koryo: 935-1392
	Hung Wu 1368-1398 Yung Lo 1403-1424	scattered Mongol tribes	Ashikaga Shogunate 1336-1573	(Mongol domination 1259-1356
	Portuguese settlement at Macao, 1557		Yoshimitsu 1367-1395	Yi Dynasty 1392 to
	Ricci in China 1582-1610		Yoshimasa 1449-1474	1910
	Benedict Goes crosses Central Asia 1602-1605		Xavier lands in Japan 1549	
		Manchus rise to power under	Nobunaga 1568-1582	Yi Dynasty
1644	Ch'ing Dynasty (Manchu) (Li Tzu-ch'eng's usurpation of the throne in 1644 is not recognized)	Nurhachi (born 1559 died 1626) Manchu Dynasty from 1636	Hideyoshi 1582-1598 Ieyasu 1600-1616 Tokugawa Shogunate 1600-1868	Japanese invasions 1592 and 1596

CHINA	NORTHERN TRIBES	JAPAN	KOREA
K'ang Hsi 1662-1722			
Ch'ien Lung 1736-1795			
"Opium Wars" 1839-1842 1856-1860		Commodore Perry lands 1853	
Taiping Rebellion 1850-1864		Meiji Restoration 1868	
Tzu Hsi (Empress Dowager) Regencies from 1861-1908			
Sino-Japanese War 1894		Sino-Japanese War 1894	
Boxer Rebellion 1900		Russo-Japanese War 1904-1905	Japanese Annexation 1910
1911-1912 Republic of China			
Revolution October, 1911		Emperor Meiji dies 1912	
Republican Gov't. proclaimed January 1, 1912			

GLOSSARY

All Under Heaven *(T'ien Hsia)*	The Chinese empire; the world
Barbarians	The term generally applied by the Chinese to all foreigners, especially the nomad tribes north of the Great Wall
Bannerman	One who belonged to one of the different Banners under which the Manchus grouped their forces
Chinese Classics, The	The Five Classics of ancient China are: "The Spring and Autumn Annals," written by Confucius; "The Book of History"; "The Book of Poetry"; the "I Li, or Book of Rituals"; and the "I Ching, or Book of Changes"
Chinoiserie	Chinese objects or Chinese styles adopted by the West
Concessions	Areas of land in some of the Chinese Treaty Ports which were leased in perpetuity by foreign governments, and in which their nationals lived
Concubine	A secondary, but legitimate wife
Daimyo *(Great Names)*	Japanese feudal lords, often virtually independent

Dynasty	A line of hereditary rulers; or the period covered by the rule of an imperial family
Extraterritoriality (sometimes abbreviated to Extrality)	The right of foreign nationals to live by their own laws and be judged by their own courts rather than by those of the country in which they are resident
Feng-shui (Wind-water)	A Chinese magical system of locating buildings, tombs and so forth in relation to their natural surroundings—hills, lakes, the points of the compass, etc.—in order to attract favorable influences
Floating World (Ukiyo)	The life of Japanese city-dwellers about the 18th century, so described because it was a life of passing things, devoted largely to pleasure and amusement
Han'gul (Korean Letters)	The phonetic system of writing the Korean language
Hermit Kingdom	Korea
Hong	The Chinese firms licensed to trade with the West in Canton
Inner Courts	The women's apartments in the Chinese imperial palace
Jesuits	Members of the Society of Jesus, founded by Ignatius Loyola in 1533, many of whom were active in China and Japan
Jinrikisha (sometimes Rickshaw)	A two-wheeled, light-weight vehicle pulled by a man; first used in Japan
Kimono	The national dress of the Japanese; a long, loose garment, crossing over in front, and held at the waist by a sash

Glossary

Mandate of Heaven	The authority from Heaven by which the Chinese emperor was believed to hold power
Middle Kingdom	China
Most-favored Nation Clause	A clause inserted in trade treaties, according to which any privilege granted to one country must be extended to all other countries having treaty relations
Old Buddha	An affectionate nickname for the Empress Dowager Tzu Hsi (1835-1908)
Onmun (Vernacular writing)	The phonetic system of writing the Korean language; later known as Han'gul
Open Door Policy	A policy suggested by the United States late in the 19th century to prevent other countries from obtaining exclusive privileges for themselves in China
Rites Controversy	A dispute in the Roman Catholic Church as to whether Christianity was or was not compatible with Confucianism, especially in regard to ancestor worship
Ronin (Wave-men)	Samurai who for some reason were not in the service of any one feudal lord
Samurai	In Japan, originally a retainer; later generally used for the military class as a whole
San Min Chu-i (Three Principles of the people)	Democracy; Nationalism; and Socialism; The Three Principles of the Chinese Republican Party which came to power as a result of the 1911 Revolution
Secret Societies	Underground organizations—religious, political, or both—which have been active at various times in Chinese history, generally opposed to and plotting against the ruling dynasty

Shinto (*The Way of the Gods*)	The native religion of Japan before the introduction of Buddhism
Shogun	Originally Sei-i Tai Shogun, "Barbarian-quelling General," an ancient Japanese military title which was revived in 1192 to denote the supreme commander. Thereafter the Shoguns were the real rulers of Japan until the Restoration of the Emperor in 1868
Shogunate	A line of hereditary Shoguns
Son of Heaven	The Emperor of China
Treaty Ports	Ports which were opened to foreign trade and foreign residents as a result of the various "unequal treaties" concluded during the 19th century
Unequal Treaties	A number of treaties between Western powers and East Asian countries concluded during the 19th century, beginning with the Treaty of Nanking in 1842, by which the countries, especially China, were forced to yield certain concessions (such as the right to trade at various ports, extraterritoriality, etc.) to the Western nations
Yangban (*Two groups*)	The two branches, civil and military, of the upper class in Korea
Zen (*in Chinese*, Ch'an)	A Buddhist sect of meditation

BIBLIOGRAPHY

(EAST ASIA: 1400 to 1912)

ARLINGTON, L. C, & LEWISOHN, WILLIAM, *In Search of Old Peking*, Henri Vetch, Peking, 1935

BACKHOUSE, E. & BLAND, J. O. P., *Annals & Memoirs of the Court of Peking*, William Heinemann, London, 1914

———, *China under the Empress Dowager*, William Heinemann, London, 1911

BALLARD, VICE-ADMIRAL G. A., *The Influence of the Sea on the Political History of Japan*, E. P. Dutton, New York, 1921

BARR, PAT, *The Coming of the Barbarians*, Macmillan & Co., Ltd. London, 1967

———, *The Deer Cry Pavilion*, Harcourt Brace & World, Inc. New York, 1968

BENEDICT, RUTH, *The Chrysanthemum and the Sword: Patterns of Japanese Culture*, Houghton Mifflin Co., Boston, 1962

BERNARD HENRI, *Le Frere Bento de Goes chez les Musulmans de la Haute Asie (1603-07)*, Hautes Etudes, Tientsin, 1934

———, *Matteo Ricci's Scientific Contribution to China*, Henri Vetch, Peking, 1935

BOXER, CHARLES R., *Jan Compagnie in Japan, 1600-1817*, Martinus Nijhoff, The Hague, 1936

———, *The Portuguese Seaborne Empire, 1415-1825*, Hutchinson & Co., Ltd., London, 1969

CARTER, DAGNEY, *China Magnificent*, John Day Co., New York, 1935

CHAMBERLAIN, BASIL HALL, *Things Japanese*, Kegan, Paul, Trench, Trubner & Co., Ltd., London, 1927 (revised from edition of 1905). (Reprinted as *Japanese Things* by Charles E. Tuttle Co., Rutland, Vermont, in 1971)

CRONIN, VINCENT, *The Wise Man from the West*, E. P. Dutton, New York, 1955

FAIRBANK, J. K. (see also Reischauer), *The United States and China*, Harvard University Press, Cambridge, 1958

FITZGERALD, C. P., *A Concise History of East Asia*, William Heinemann, London, 1966

——, *The Horizon History of China*, American Heritage Publishing Co., Inc. New York, 1969

FLEMING, PETER, *The Siege at Peking*, Rupert Hart-Davis, London 1959

GOODRICH, L. C., *A Short History of the Chinese People*, George Allen & Unwin, London, 1957

HATADA, TAKASHI, *A History of Korea* (Translated and edited by Warren W. Smith, Jr. and Benjamin H. Hazard), Clio Press, Santa Barbara, California, 1969

HERRMANN, ALBERT, *An Historical Atlas of China*, Edinburgh University Press, 1966 (or Aldine Publishing Co., Chicago)

HUDSON, G. F., *Europe and China*, Edward Arnold, London, 1931

——, *The Far East in Politics*, Oxford University Press, 1937

HUMMEL, A. W., *Eminent Chinese of the Ch'ing Period*, U. S. Government Printing Office, Washington, 1943

HURD, DOUGLAS, *The Arrow War*, Collins, London, 1967

KENNEDY, MALCOLM, *A Short History of Japan*, Mentor Books, New York, 1963

LATOURETTE, KENNETH, *The Chinese, Their History and Culture* The Macmillan Co., New York 1934

——, *The History of Japan*, The Macmillan Co., New York, 1957

——, *A History of Modern China*, Pelican Books, London, 1954

LEGGE, JAMES, *The Sacred Books of China* (5 vols.), Oxford University Press, 1879

Bibliography

LIN, YUTANG, *Imperial Peking*, Elek Books, Ltd., London, 1961

McCUNE, EVELYN, *The Arts of Korea*, Charles E. Tuttle Co., Rutland, Vermont, 1962

McCUNE, GEORGE, *Korea Today*, Harvard University Press, Cambridge, 1950

NEEDHAM, JOSEPH, *Science and Civilisation in China* (Volume I), Cambridge University Press, England, 1954

OSGOOD, CORNELIUS, *The Koreans and their Culture*, Ronald Press, New York, 1951

POLO, MARCO, *Description of the World* (Translated as *The Travels of Marco Polo* by R. E. Latham) Penguin Books, London, 1958

REISCHAUER, EDWIN O. & FAIRBANK, J. K., *East Asia: The Great Tradition*, Vol. I of "A History of East Asian Civilization," Houghton Mifflin Co., Boston, 1960

REISCHAUER, EDWIN O., FAIRBANK, J. K. & CRAIG, ALBERT M., *East Asia: The Modern Transformation*, Vol. II of *A History of East Asian Civilization*, Houghton Mifflin Co., Boston, 1964

REICHWEIN, ADOLF, *China and Europe*, Routledge & Kegan Paul, London, 1968

SANSOM, SIR GEORGE, *Japan: A Short Cultural History*, The Cresset Press, London, 1931

———, *A History of Japan, 1334-1615*, Stanford University Press, 1961

———, *The Western World and Japan*, The Cresset Press, London, 1950

STORRY, RICHARD, *A History of Modern Japan*, Cassell & Co., London, 1962

———, *Japan* Oxford University Press (in "Modern World Series"), 1965

TSAO, HSUEH-CHIN, *Dream of the Red Chamber* (Translated by Chi-Chen Wang), Doubleday & Co., New York, 1958

WILLETTS, WILLIAM, *Chinese Art* (2 vols.), Penguin Books, London, 1958

WU CH'ENG-EN, *Monkey* (Translated by Arthur Waley), George Allen & Unwin, London, 1942

Index

Index

Index